BEST OF THE BEST PRESENTS

FOODS YOU CRAVE
The Low-Carb Way

GEORGE STELLA

WITH **CHRISTIAN STELLA**

QUAIL RIDGE PRESS
Preserving America's Food Heritage

Authors:
George Stella
with Christian Stella

Book Design and Food Photography by
Christian and Elise Stella

This book is not meant to dispense medical advice. Please consult your doctor before making any dramatic changes to the way you eat.

Nutritional analysis provided on each recipe is meant only as a reference and has been compiled to the best of our ability using nutritional analysis software. Due to differences in sizes, brands, and types of ingredients, your calculations may vary. Calories have been rounded to the nearest 5, and all other amounts were rounded to the nearest .5 of a gram.

Library of Congress Cataloging-in-Publication Data

Names: Stella, George, author. | Stella, Christian, author.
Title: Best of the best presents : foods you crave : the low-carb way / George Stella with Christian Stella.
Description: First edition. | Brandon, MS : Quail Ridge Press, 2018. | Includes index. | "Preserving America's Food Heritage."
Identifiers: LCCN 2017050142 | ISBN 9781938879241
Subjects: LCSH: Low-carbohydrate diet--Recipes. | LCGFT: Cookbooks.
Classification: LCC RM237.73 .S742 2018 | DDC 641.5/6383--dc23
LC record available at https://lccn.loc.gov/2017050142

ISBN 978-1-938879-24-1
Printed in the United States of America
First printing, January 2018

QUAIL RIDGE PRESS
P. O. Box 123 • Brandon, MS 39043 • 1-800-343-1583
info@quailridge.com • www.quailridge.com

FOODS YOU CRAVE

The Low-Carb Way

Moo Shu Shrimp, *page 117*

CONTENTS YOU CRAVE

Finding the Low-Carb Way

INTRODUCTION

Food has always been my greatest passion in life, whether it was good for me or not. Food has always been tied to my evolving career—from chef, to "celebrity" chef on the Food Network, to cookbook author. I work with food every single day because I truly love food. Who doesn't? Who doesn't crave comfort foods? Who wouldn't crave "comfort"? Maybe it's the middle of the night and all you want is a chocolate brownie or two. Or maybe you're staring at a menu and your eye is wandering away from the boring salads and toward the chicken pot pie, or the meatloaf, or the chocolate brownies....

We're all hardwired to have those cravings. As someone who was once 467 pounds, I know a thing or two about food cravings. My life revolved around eating and I was always craving more.

I was also suffering through numerous health problems, including congestive heart failure, sleep apnea, and multiple bouts of pneumonia. I was confined to a wheelchair and doctors had told me that I was going to die.

My family had been steadily gaining weight alongside me. We had become a fat family, enabling each other in our bad eating. My wife Rachel—who had never struggled with her weight earlier in life—had reached 200 pounds. My two teenage sons were gaining more and more weight every year, with my youngest son Christian reaching 305 pounds at age 15. We all seemed to be resigned to the way things were going, and the size we had become.

We found out about low-carb eating at the perfect moment, when both my health and

morale were at their lowest, when my whole family was spiraling down alongside me. Low-carb seemed like a long shot at first. It allowed us to eat many of the foods we already craved, but more importantly, it didn't feel like a dreaded "diet." We didn't feel hungry or like we had to count every single bite of food that we ate.

As a chef working in some of Florida's best restaurants, I had always loved to cook. The downside of being a chef is that you don't always want to come home and fire up the grill

BEFORE

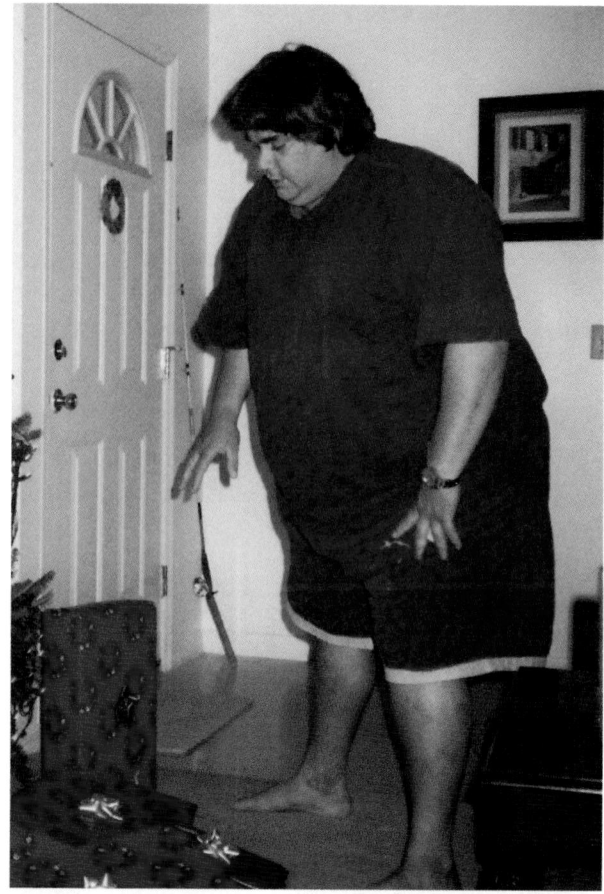

AFTER

after 12 hours of cooking over a commercial grill. Once my health had deteriorated, I wasn't cooking at home or in a restaurant. I simply wasn't cooking at all. Low-carb gave me back my passion for cooking. It gave me the drive to cook for my family—and for myself—food of the quality I once cooked only for restaurant guests.

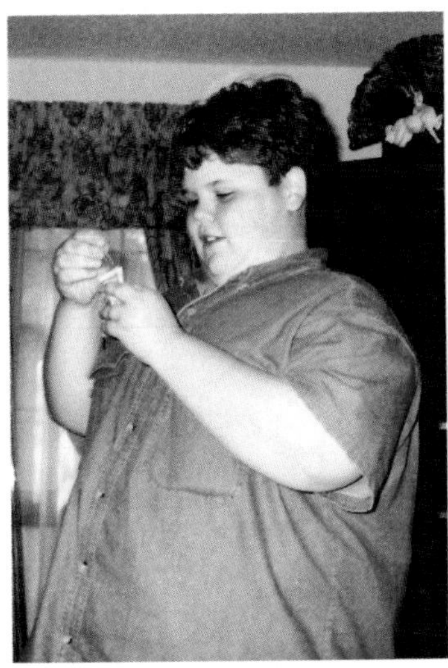

I soon learned that low-carb wasn't a "diet" at all. It was a lifestyle, and one I had no problem sticking to...a lifestyle my whole family adopted together...a lifestyle change with real results...results that start in the kitchen, cooking fresh and delicious meals made from real food. To eat well, you have to cook well. It doesn't have to be difficult. And it doesn't have to take all day.

True success can only come when you're enjoying the journey. Cooking should never feel like work, and eating should never be boring. You don't want to be left craving food, but instead, feel like you are always eating the foods that you crave.

For us, success came quickly. My family lost over 560 pounds, and have kept it off for more than 13 years. Rachel and Anthony each dropped over 70 pounds. Christian lost more than half his body weight, going from 305 to under 150. I lost 265 pounds, got out of the wheelchair, and was finally back in restaurant kitchens—only this time I didn't do all the cooking in the workplace.

I wasn't just cooking at home; I was developing new dishes. I was reinventing comfort foods to fit into our low-carb lifestyle. My family never felt like we had to go without, and we kept perfecting our recipes every day of our weight loss.

It has been over a decade since my first cookbook of low-carb recipes was published, and we're still in the kitchen cooking. We're still living a low-carb lifestyle and loving every minute of it. We're still developing brand new recipes and perfecting old techniques.

When I set out to write this, my ninth (even

I can't believe that) low-carb cookbook, I asked myself which foods do I crave the most, and which of those have I never been able to recreate for our lifestyle? Then I worked and worked to find a way...to find the low-carb way to make these classic comfort foods...to finally satisfy those cravings for all types of foods. Yes! Even brownies!

HOW LOW-CARB WORKS

First and foremost, I am a chef, not a doctor, nutritionist, or scientist. My experiments are with ingredients, not test tubes. The good news is—this is a cookbook! You wouldn't want a doctor writing recipes (many have), but you should consult a doctor or nutritionist before making changes to the way you eat.

You should also understand that my explanation of how low-carb works is extremely simplified and based on my own experience of losing weight. The specifics of what is actually happening inside the body to lead to weight loss is beyond the scope of this cookbook, but something you may want to further research. I would highly suggest *Dr. Atkins' New Diet Revolution*, as that is the book that we read before starting our own personal journeys. It's very long, very technical, but pretty much the go-to reference book on low-carb by the man who started it all, Robert Atkins.

That said, here is my simplification of why and how low-carb works.

STORING FAT

The concept of eating low-carb is actually quite simple to explain. Our bodies are capable of converting either carbohydrates or fat into the energy needed to function; however, our bodies prefer carbohydrates when they are available. Eating a diet full of carbohydrates causes the body to burn only the carbs necessary to get through the day before then converting the remaining carbohydrates into fat, which is then stored—alongside the actual fat you eat—in the event there ever comes a time when excess fat is needed for survival. This is the reason that overeating leads to weight gain. When eating an abundance of carbohydrates alongside fat, we are similar to bears storing fat for hibernation in the winter.

BURNING FAT

Your body can also create energy from fat when it is not supplied with an ample amount of carbohydrates. By converting fat into energy, your body goes into a constant fat-burning state known as "ketosis." Not only do you burn the fat that you eat, you can also burn through your reserved fat. Most people find it hard to grasp why low-carb allows you to eat fattier foods. There's a simple explanation—your body burns it right off.

Entering the "ketosis" state is easily achieved; simply stop eating processed carbohydrates. If you are looking to lose weight, staying in a state of ketosis is important to success. Cheating on a low-carb lifestyle will take your body out of ketosis and stop burning fat.

For me, the best judge of whether my body was in ketosis, was whether I was losing weight from week to week (don't weigh yourself daily or you'll go crazy). That said, you can also purchase very inexpensive test strips at most pharmacies or superstores. They will be labeled as "ketone test strips," as they measure the ketones in your body. Some blood sugar meters can also measure ketones. Testing is really unnecessary unless you have stalled on losing weight. In that instance, you can use these test strips alongside eliminating specific foods to determine whether a food you are eating is knocking you out of ketosis.

THE LOW-CARB LIFESTYLE

I refer to low-carb as a "lifestyle," as it works best when you eliminate processed carbohydrates completely, without cheating. This is how you achieve ketosis full-time for the maximum benefit.

If you have a lot of weight to lose, I'd highly suggest you go all-in on low-carb. Embrace the lifestyle and eat great tasting, fresh foods every day. It absolutely changed my life and the lives of my family.

FOODS TO AVOID

You can't succeed on low-carb if you don't know which high-carb foods to avoid. Refined grains, sugars, and starches—otherwise known as "the white stuff"—are not a part of a low-carb lifestyle. This includes:

- Flour and all wheat products (bread, pasta, cereal, crackers)
- Sugar (all types, including honey and maple syrup)
- White potatoes and potato products
- Corn products (including cornstarch)
- High-sugar fruits (bananas, mangos, grapes, watermelon, etc.)
- Fruit juice
- Beans
- Milk (cream is fine, but milk has more lactose, which is a form of sugar)

READ THE LABELS

No matter how hard I've tried, I can't completely avoid some packaged food items (such as tomato sauce or paste). When buying anything with a nutritional label, always read the ingredients! Food manufacturers hide sugar and starches in just about anything they can. If you can't make something yourself, you should at least be aware of what is in it.

Simply checking the carb counts on the label is usually not enough, as some products can fall below certain levels (especially products with very small serving sizes), and claim they have zero carbohydrates, even if they contain sugar. A good example of this is non-dairy coffee creamers. They are usually pretty low in carbs, yet they usually contain mostly high-fructose corn syrup and partially-hydrogenated vegetable oil—also known as trans-fat.

KICKING THE CARB CRAVINGS

Everyone gets food cravings, whether you are watching your weight or otherwise. These cravings are often for carbohydrates, as they are often the quickest way to get the densest number of calories into your body. When you aren't eating low-carb, they are your body's preferred fuel source, so you're practically hardwired to crave carbohydrates.

The problem is, that when you switch to a low-carb lifestyle, your body doesn't quite catch on to that, and you will likely continue to crave carbs. Likely, you'll have moments where you'll crave them more than you ever did before. The heart grows fonder for what it can't, or at least shouldn't, have!

So what can you do? It may be the middle of the afternoon and you're craving a big bowl of carbs topped with a few more carbs, but don't throw in the towel. To kick the carb habit, you've got to kick the cravings.

These are a few of the ways my family and I dealt with our own carb cravings:

CLEAN OUT THE CUPBOARDS

Low-carb works best when the whole household is on board (though Rachel and I did successfully start low-carb a few months before our own kids). If no one in your household is eating carbs, then there is no reason to have any stocked in your pantry, fridge, or freezer. Be sure to clean everything out, donating or giving away any high-carb food when possible, so that there simply aren't any carbs in the house to tempt you.

COOK WHEN YOU CRAVE

Physical activity is one of the best ways to preoccupy your mind. It is only natural then, that when you are craving high-carb foods, the mere act of cooking a low-carb alternative can help distract you from those cravings. We also tend to enjoy food more when we've worked to make it. So, while you may not be cooking that big bowl of carbs you were craving, the fact that you made something from scratch will give you much of that same satisfaction you were looking for.

STOCK SATISFYING SNACKS

For those times when you simply do not have the time to cook, you'll want to make sure that you have some kind of snack that you can simply grab and go. A high protein snack filled with heart-healthy fats will satisfy your hunger and should hold you over until your next meal. Many of the snack recipes in this book can be prepared in advance and stored for several days for just these occasions. Some good store-bought options include:

- Nuts and seeds
- String cheese
- Salami or pepperoni
- Hardboiled eggs
- Olives
- Avocados

But the best low-carb snack of all is usually... Leftovers! We always cook extra and stock the fridge with leftovers for the days ahead.

DON'T SHOP HUNGRY

I always advocate shopping the outer aisles of your grocery store, as that is where the fresh foods are kept. You'll want to venture into the inner aisles with packaged food products as little as possible, but you'll inevitably have to venture in there for some things. In those instances, be sure you never shop on an empty stomach! Food companies have marketing departments for a reason, and packaging is designed to tempt you. Fill your stomach before you fill your cart and you'll be less tempted to slip back into old shopping habits.

EAT MORE FULFILLING MEALS

If you are craving carbs at a certain point in the day, try eating a higher amount of protein in your meals earlier in the day. This may help you feel full and satisfied longer.

LOOK FOR TRIGGER FOODS

Evaluate whether any food you are eating is a "trigger" food that is causing you to crave more carbohydrates. For my family, we can eat fresh berries on low-carb without any problem, but other people may get more cravings after eating them, as they do contain natural carbohydrates. Be especially cautious of any store-bought products that are labeled as low-carb, foods like "low-carb" pastas, breads, snacks, and candies. If it tastes too good to be true, it likely is, and may disrupt any weight loss and leave you craving more and more carbohydrates. This is why we never recommend low-carb products. We tried several products when we first started out and they always stalled our weight loss.

THINK OF THE FINISH LINE

I often write my cookbooks with the assumption that the reader is living a long-term low-carb lifestyle. Rachel and I have been living low-carb for over fifteen years now and still eat low-carb full time. That being said, there are many people who have success on low-carb, and then go on to reintroduce carbs back into their diet. Christian lost 160 pounds between the ages of 15 and 18, but then slowly started eating more carbs when he met his wife Elise, who did not have a weight problem. He has still managed to keep his weight off by eating a carb-conscious lifestyle for the past decade. If you get a craving, it doesn't mean you can never eat that food again, but you'll be happier to eat it once you've reached your goal.

ABOUT SUGAR SUBSTITUTES

As sugar is a carbohydrate, you can't eat low-carb without cutting out all types of real sugar, including sucrose, glucose, corn syrup, high-fructose corn syrup, added fructose, cane juice, cane syrup, and honey. But once you've cut these things out of your diet, you're inevitably still going to want to indulge in something sweet. You're going to have to find a substitution.

Sugar substitutes are a polarizing topic that has been, and continues to be debated in the news, on the web, and elsewhere. Opinions vary about the different varieties of sugar substitutes, and seem to change too often to keep up with. It is only natural for us to question and, yes, even demand more information on what we put into our bodies. Sugar substitutes often cause people to wonder what is or isn't naturally derived, and for those conscious of eating only natural foods (as we try to do on low-carb), this is wholly understandable.

As a chef, I tend to vote with my palate. It was over a decade ago that I chose to use Splenda as my personal sugar substitute of choice, and have stuck with it ever since. This is simply my own preference due to taste and the fact that it didn't interfere with my weight loss. However, your choice of sugar substitute or "sugar alternative" is left entirely up to you.

THE NEW SUBSTITUTES

There is a remarkable amount of sugar substitutes available in stores today, many of them entirely natural. This luxury simply did not exist back when my family lost the majority of our weight. Back then, Splenda had just hit the shelves and any other alternatives came in either blue or pink packets. These days, you have a plethora of new substitutes to choose from, including erythritol, stevia, monk fruit, and agave nectar, just to name a few. Others are marketed under many different brand names, such as Nevella, Truvia, Stevia Blend, Swerve, Organic Zero, EZ-Sweetz, and Just Like Sugar. The one type of sugar substitute I recommend against is xylitol, as, from what I understand, it can cause digestive discomfort (and is also poisonous to dogs).

DO THEY CAUSE WEIGHT GAIN?

Lately, you may have read that sugar substitutes can actually lead to weight gain. This seems to be the sensational story that is spread around the most right now. My only response to that is that my family consumed Splenda throughout our weight loss (and we still do), and it never slowed us down! We ate desserts just like those in this book, made of the same ingredients (these exact recipes had not been developed yet) every day of our weight loss, and we had amazing results. Today, we eat the exact desserts in this book to maintain our weight.

It's important to remember that sugar substitutes are among some of the most scrutinized and studied foods on the planet. When in doubt, read these studies and the conclusions of those who publish them, then draw your own conclusion. I made mine long ago and feel comfortable knowing that I've eliminated both sugar and corn syrup from my life.

It is generally well accepted that eating excess sugar can raise your risk for diabetes and other diseases, especially for those who are overweight. The media likes to sensationalize sweeteners, but real sugar (and especially high-fructose corn syrup) is not good for those who are overweight.

MAKE SURE IT'S HEAT STABLE

Regardless of your preference in sweeteners, please check to make sure it is "heat stable" before attempting to bake with it. Aspartame, for instance, (which I do NOT recommend) is not heat stable and will lose its sweetness at a high enough temperature.

The recipes in this book which call for sugar substitute are all measured equal to sugar in order to make them easy to follow, no matter which substitute you prefer. If you are using a brand of sugar substitute that does not measure the same as sugar, simply follow the directions on the package to measure out the correct amount for that particular brand.

Liquid versions of sweeteners listed tend to contain the least amount of carbohydrates, as they require no fillers to add bulk. These also usually measure the least like sugar, so be sure to follow their directions for measuring!

REAL SUGAR...REALLY

Finally, I would like to mention one final option. If you have purchased this book with the goal to eat less or no gluten, and not to watch your weight, you can make the choice to use real sugar in my recipes. In the past, I have noticed that many people buy my books purely because of gluten allergies or sensitivities. In this case—if you happen to have no issue with weight, are not at risk for diabetes, and feel comfortable with eating sugar—by all means do so.

Your choice of sweetener is truly your choice to make.

ABOUT THE RECIPES

When I cook, I try to keep things as simple as possible. When I write recipes, I try to make them easy to follow and use only ingredients that we can find at our local grocery store, as well as the big box superstore. I try to include tips whenever an ingredient needs more explanation. I also include nutritional information to help you make the right choices for your particular diet.

That said, there are some questions you may still have about my recipes, so I've included this section to explain a few unique ingredients, and break down how we've calculated our nutritional information.

ALMOND FLOUR

Many brands of almond flour can now be purchased in most grocery stores and are usually found in the baking, organic, or gluten-free sections. They have now come down in price as well, and can often be found for less money per pound than whole almonds. Once opened, almond flour should be resealed and stored in the freezer to stay fresh.

You can also prepare your own almond flour: Simply grind sliced, slivered, or whole raw almonds in a food processor on high for about 3 minutes. Once they've attained a grainy, flour-like consistency, keep stored in an airtight container in the freezer. For an even lighter, fluffier flour, grind small batches of almonds in a coffee grinder.

Blanched almonds are recommended, as they are white and have no hull, making for cleaner "white" flour-like baked goods. Most store-bought almond flour is made from blanched almonds.

Whole almonds, out of the shell, but with the hull, will make for speckled brown baked goods. There are at least two brands that sell premade almond flour like this and they are usually labeled as "natural almond flour." We recommend this type for only one recipe in this book, our Carrot Bar Cake, recipe page 207. This recommendation is purely for looks though, and has nothing to do with the flavor.

While almonds do contain fat (something that white flour does not), this fat happens to be the good (monounsaturated) kind and doesn't deserve to be sneered at. Our baked goods, at first glance, might seem high in fat due to our use of almond flour, though these numbers hold little importance when you take into consideration where the fat comes from. Some studies have even shown that a serving of almonds a day can help boost weight loss.

COCONUT FLOUR

Coconut flour is made only out of coconut, and used in a select few recipes in this book. It can usually be found in the baking, organic, or gluten-free section of your grocery store.

Coconut flour cannot be substituted in place of almond flour in the other recipes in this book, as coconut flour needs a LOT of liquid to hydrate it. It's almost closer to cornstarch than flour, which is why we only use it sparingly to give something a denser texture.

NUTRITIONAL INFORMATION

The nutritional analysis provided in these recipes is meant only as a reference. It was compiled to the best of our ability using nutritional analysis software with an extremely large database of ingredients. Due to variance in the sizes of vegetables, brands of certain foods, or fat content of meat, your calculations may vary.

Calculations are for each serving of the finished dish. Calories in this book were rounded to the nearest 5, and all other amounts were rounded to the nearest .5 of a gram. Optional garnishes or variations were not included in the calculations. Recipes that include the use of another recipe (such as Pulled Pork Picnic in a Jar, recipe page 39) already include the nutritional information for the additional recipe as part of the overall dish.

Though we have provided this nutritional information, our family has always made it a point to not count each and every gram of carbohydrates or calories. It is our belief that if you stock your home full of great natural foods and do your best to not "cheat," you'll be eating well enough to see results. I've found that, for many people, counting carbs can lead you to eat worse when trying to save up or "bank" those extra carbs in order to eat something you probably shouldn't be eating at all. Starving yourself all day to eat an entire pie before bedtime has and never will be a good choice.

We suggest you set yourself free from those numbers altogether, and eat only what is essential for success. Yeah, we know, we know, it is a tough urge to let go of, but trust us—it'll do wonders for your sanity! Get too caught up with counting, and eventually you may find yourself doing long division on the walls.

NET CARBS

You will notice a number labeled "Net Carbs" in our nutritional information. Net carbs are the carbohydrates that are actually absorbed by your body—the ones that actually affect your blood sugar levels. If you are counting carbs, net carbs are the ones to count.

Our net carbs are determined only by subtracting fiber from the total carbohydrates in the recipe, as fiber does not get absorbed. Food products and other books subtract other things, such as "sugar alcohols," but we ONLY subtract fiber to come up with our net carbs.

FIVE-INGREDIENT RECIPES

There are many five-ingredient recipes labeled throughout this book. I did not set out to write a five-ingredient cookbook, but I do naturally try to keep many of my recipes as simple as possible. When we decided to label these recipes with a symbol, we asked ourselves what should constitute an "ingredient" to count toward the limit of five. There are certain pantry staples that are just too common to count, so we did not count them toward the five ingredients. These ingredients are salt, pepper, sugar substitute, vegetable oil, and nonstick cooking spray. I've seen other five-ingredient recipes purposefully leave out something as essential as salt, simply to hit that arbitrary number. My five-ingredient recipes should only need you to shop for five ingredients or less, as you likely already have nonstick cooking spray or salt in the house.

The following is a list of the most commonly used ingredients in our recipes and in our household. We try to keep most of these ingredients on hand at all times.

SPICE CABINET

- Baking powder
- Balsamic vinegar
- Bay leaves
- Black pepper
- Chili powder
- Cider vinegar
- Cinnamon
- Coconut extract
- Cumin
- Food coloring
- Garlic powder
- Italian seasoning
- Nonstick cooking spray
- Olive oil
- Onion powder
- Oregano
- Paprika
- Smoked paprika
- Thyme
- Vanilla extract
- Vegetable oil

PANTRY

- Almond flour
- Baking chocolate, unsweetened
- Beef stock
- Chicken stock
- Cocoa powder, unsweetened
- Coconut flour
- Dijon mustard
- Flax seed, milled
- Garlic, minced
- Pecans, chopped
- Red onions
- Sugar substitute
- Worcestershire sauce
- Yellow onions

FRIDGE

- Bacon
- Bell peppers
- Butter
- Cauliflower
- Cilantro
- Cream cheese
- Eggs, large
- Fresh herbs
- Half-and-half
- Heavy cream
- Lemons
- Limes
- Mayonnaise
- Parmesan cheese
- Parsley
- Zucchini

BREAKFAST

five ingredient recipe ✋

PREP TIME: 20 MIN • COOK TIME: 35 MIN • SERVES: 6

CHICKEN SAUSAGE BREAKFAST CASSEROLE

This casserole with smoked chicken sausage, broccoli, and sharp Cheddar cheese is big enough to feed a real crowd, or at least 6 very hungry individuals. You can even prep it the night before, cover, refrigerate, and easily pop it in the oven the next morning. It's the perfect way to handle breakfast for overnight houseguests.

SHOPPING LIST

Nonstick cooking spray

1 tablespoon butter

1 package (4–5 links) smoked chicken sausage, sliced

1/2 cup diced yellow onion

12 ounces frozen broccoli florets, thawed

2 cups sharp Cheddar cheese

12 large eggs

1/2 cup heavy cream

1/2 teaspoon salt

1/4 teaspoon pepper

HELPFUL TIPS

The smoked chicken sausage in this recipe is the kind that is sold fully cooked, near the hot dogs in the grocery store. Any flavor will do, but be on the lookout for a brand without added sugar.

1. Preheat oven to 375°F. Spray a 13x9-inch baking dish with nonstick cooking spray.
2. Melt the butter in a skillet over medium-high heat.
3. Add the chicken sausage and onion to the skillet and sauté 5 minutes, or until sausage begins to brown and onions are translucent. Transfer to the prepared baking dish.
4. Squeeze the thawed broccoli florets to remove excess water, then pat dry with paper towels. Transfer to the baking dish.
5. Add the Cheddar cheese to the baking dish and toss to disperse all ingredients.
6. In a large mixing bowl, whisk eggs with heavy cream, salt, and pepper. Pour over all ingredients in the baking dish.
7. Bake 35 minutes, or until the center of the casserole is springy to the touch and top is beginning to brown. Let cool 5 minutes before slicing.

Calories: 480 • Fat: 37g • Protein: 31g • Total Carbs: 5g - Fiber: 2g = Net Carbs: 3g

PREP TIME: 5 MIN • COOK TIME: 10 MIN • SERVES: 2

LOW-CARB "OATMEAL"

While I far prefer almond flour for baked goods, coconut flour makes for this wonderful low-carb breakfast porridge. Serve topped with your favorite toppings, such as fresh berries, chopped nuts, cinnamon, or a swirl of cream.

SHOPPING LIST

1 1/4 cups unsweetened almond milk
1/3 cup coconut flour
3 tablespoons sugar substitute
1/2 teaspoon maple extract
1/4 teaspoon ground cinnamon
1 large egg, beaten

HELPFUL TIPS

Unsweetened coconut or soy milk can be used in place of the almond milk to make this nut-free.

1 Heat almond milk, coconut flour, sugar substitute, maple extract, and cinnamon in a sauce pot over medium-high heat, just until it begins to bubble.

2 Reduce heat to low and let cook, stirring constantly, for 2 minutes.

3 Remove the pot from the heat and slowly whisk the egg into the "oatmeal," whisking as you add the egg to keep it from cooking before it can be incorporated.

4 Return to the heat and cook, stirring constantly, an additional 3 minutes.

5 Remove from heat and let rest 5 minutes, to soften, before serving. Serve warm.

Calories: 155 • Fat: 7.5g • Protein: 6.5g • Total Carbs: 14.5g - Fiber: 7.5g = **Net Carbs: 7g**

PREP TIME: 10 MIN • COOK TIME: 30 MIN • SERVES: 6

MUSHROOM SWISS EGG MUFFINS

Baked scrambled egg muffins make for a quick grab-and-go breakfast that you can prepare in advance and enjoy for up to three days. Personally, I think they taste even better cold!

SHOPPING LIST

Nonstick cooking spray

1 tablespoon butter

8 ounces baby bella mushrooms, chopped

1 cup shredded Swiss cheese

6 large eggs

2 tablespoons heavy cream

1/4 teaspoon salt

1/4 teaspoon pepper

HELPFUL TIPS

For more color and flavor, add 1/4 cup of diced red onion to the mushrooms as you sauté them.

1. Preheat oven to 350°F. Spray a 6-cup muffin tin with nonstick cooking spray.
2. Melt the butter in a skillet over medium-high heat.
3. Add the mushrooms to the skillet and sauté 5 minutes, or until they are tender and beginning to caramelize. Drain any excess liquid and pat dry with paper towels.
4. Divide the mushrooms equally between the 6 prepared muffin cups, then top with an equal amount of the Swiss cheese.
5. In a large mixing bowl, whisk eggs with heavy cream, salt, and pepper. Pour evenly over the ingredients in each muffin cup.
6. Bake 25 minutes, or until the center of the muffins are springy to the touch. Let cool 3 minutes before removing from the muffin tin to serve.

Calories: 180 • Fat: 14g • Protein: 12g • Total Carbs: 3.5g - Fiber: 0.5g = **Net Carbs: 3g**

PREP TIME: 10 MIN • COOK TIME: 15 MIN • SERVES: 4

BREAKFAST

GUACAMOLE FRITTATA

Topped with chunks of fresh avocado and chopped cilantro, this frittata is a good excuse to have (the flavors of) guacamole for breakfast. Pepper-jack cheese is baked over the top, because to have a frittata, you've just got to have cheese!

SHOPPING LIST

1 tablespoon olive oil
1/4 cup diced red onion
1/2 teaspoon minced garlic
6 large eggs
1/4 teaspoon salt
1/4 teaspoon black pepper
1/8 teaspoon baking powder
1 avocado, chopped
2 tablespoons chopped cilantro
1/2 cup shredded pepper-jack cheese

HELPFUL TIPS

This can also be made with dollops of actual guacamole in place of the avocado, but make sure to find a brand without added sugar.

1. Preheat oven to 375°F.
2. Heat the olive oil in a large ovenproof skillet over medium heat.
3. Add the onion and garlic and sauté just until the onion is translucent, about 3 minutes.
4. In a mixing bowl, whisk together the eggs, salt, pepper, and baking powder. Pour over the onions in the skillet.
5. Using a rubber spatula, gently push the cooked egg from one side of the pan to the other to allow more of the raw egg to reach the bottom of the pan. Continue doing this until the top of the eggs are only slightly runny.
6. Arrange the chopped avocado over the runny eggs and then top all with chopped cilantro and pepper-jack cheese.
7. Bake 8–10 minutes, or until eggs have puffed up and frittata is browning around the edges. Serve immediately.

Calories: 260 • Fat: 21g • Protein: 13.5g • Total Carbs: 5.5g - Fiber: 2.5g = Net Carbs: 3g

PREP TIME: 15 MIN • BAKE TIME: 15 MIN • MAKES: 12 • SERVES: 12

GARLIC AND CHEDDAR BISCUITS

These low-carb drop biscuits are like the popular Cheddar biscuits you'd find in that popular lobster restaurant. Buttery, garlicky, and loaded with extra-sharp Cheddar cheese, these make the perfect side for any seafood recipe or picnic lunch.

SHOPPING LIST

2 cups almond flour

3/4 cup shredded extra-sharp Cheddar cheese

2 teaspoons baking powder

1/2 teaspoon salt

5 tablespoons butter, melted

2 large eggs

2 teaspoons minced garlic

Old Bay seasoning, to top

HELPFUL TIPS

Biscuits typically require cold butter to be cut into the dough, however these drop biscuits require melted butter.

1. Preheat oven to 350°F. Line a sheet pan with parchment paper.
2. In a mixing bowl, stir together almond flour, Cheddar cheese, baking powder, and salt.
3. In a separate bowl, whisk together melted butter, eggs, and garlic.
4. Fold the wet ingredients into the dry ingredients to create a dough.
5. Drop rounded tablespoons of the dough onto the prepared sheet pan and pat down to form a rounded biscuit. Lightly season the tops of the biscuits with Old Bay seasoning.
6. Bake 15 minutes, until biscuits are golden brown. Serve warm.

Calories: 190 • Fat: 17g • Protein: 7g • Total Carbs: 5g - Fiber: 2g = Net Carbs: 3g

PREP TIME: 15 MIN • BAKE TIME: 15 MIN • SERVES: 4

AVOCADO BAKED EGGS

A whole egg is baked right into the center of an avocado in this simple, all-in-one breakfast that is packed with not only protein, but heart-healthy fats. As you do need to scoop a little of the avocado out around the pit to make more room for the egg, I mash that up to make a fresh (not baked) avocado topping to go over top.

SHOPPING LIST

2 avocados

4 large eggs

Salt and pepper

1/2 teaspoon lime juice

1/4 cup diced tomato

HELPFUL TIPS

Smaller pitted avocados may require scooping more of the meat out to fit the egg. It's better to scoop too much than too little and end up with the egg overflowing out of the fruit!

1. Preheat oven to 425°F. Line a sheet pan with parchment paper.
2. Halve and pit the avocados, but do not peel them. Using a spoon, scoop an additional tablespoon or so of meat out of the center of each avocado half to make room for the eggs. Reserve the scooped avocado.
3. Place avocado halves on the prepared sheet pan and crack an egg into the center of each. Season both the egg and the avocado around it with salt and pepper.
4. Bake 15 minutes, or until the whites of the eggs have set, but yolks are still runny.
5. Meanwhile, mash lime juice into the reserved avocado.
6. Top the egg in each baked avocado with 1 tablespoon of the mashed avocado and 1 tablespoon of the diced tomato before serving.

Calories: 200 • Fat: 16.5g • Protein: 9g • Total Carbs: 8.5g - Fiber: 5g = **Net Carbs: 3.5g**

SUPER STRAWBERRY MINUTE MUFFIN

Freeze-dried strawberries are one of my new favorite ingredients to work with, as they pack so much strawberry flavor into so few carbs. A one-minute microwave mug muffin like this one could not exist without them, as fresh strawberries would release too much water as they cook, preventing the muffin from setting.

SHOPPING LIST

2 teaspoons butter

1/4 cup almond flour

1 large egg

2 tablespoons chopped freeze-dried strawberries

2 tablespoons sugar substitute

1/4 teaspoon vanilla extract

1/4 teaspoon baking powder

Pinch salt

1. Place butter in a microwave-safe mug and heat 15 seconds, just until melted.
2. Add all remaining ingredients to the mug and whisk until well combined.
3. Microwave for 1 minute on HIGH, just until batter rises in mug. It will likely rise just above the lip of the mug, then lower as you open the microwave.
4. Muffin should be springy in the center. If it has not set, microwave an additional 10 seconds, or until the muffin rises. Serve warm.

HELPFUL TIPS

Freeze-dried strawberries are usually sold in foil bags in the produce section or alongside the raisins in the grocery store. The ingredients should include no added sugar.

Calories: 205 • Fat: 16g • Protein: 8g • Total Carbs: 7.5g - Fiber: 2g = Net Carbs: 5.5g

EGGPLANT CAPONATA HASH

While true Caponata is actually an eggplant salad from Sicily, I find that the Italian flavors make for a unique and interesting breakfast diversion. For a full meal, serve topped with fried or poached eggs.

SHOPPING LIST

2 tablespoons olive oil

1 eggplant, cut into 3/4-inch cubes

1/3 cup diced yellow onion

1/4 cup diced red bell pepper

1 teaspoon minced garlic

1/2 teaspoon paprika

1/4 teaspoon salt

1/4 teaspoon pepper

1/4 cup chopped fresh basil

2 teaspoons balsamic vinegar

1. Heat olive oil in a large skillet over medium-high heat, until nearly smoking hot.
2. Add all ingredients, except basil and vinegar, to the skillet and stir to coat eggplant in the spices.
3. Cook, stirring very infrequently, about 10 minutes, or until eggplant is tender and many of the pieces have browned. If the eggplant is not browning, raise the heat to high and stir less frequently.
4. Stir in basil and balsamic vinegar before serving.

HELPFUL TIPS

Though this recipe does not call for them, Caponata is typically made with capers. For a more authentic take on the dish, simply add 2 tablespoons of drained and rinsed capers in the last step.

Calories: 100 • Fat: 7.5g • Protein: 1.5g • Total Carbs: 9g - Fiber: 4.5g = Net Carbs: 4.5g

PREP TIME: 10 MIN • COOK TIME: 55 MIN • SERVES: 6

FRENCH ONION QUICHE

French onion soup is one of those things that is hard to translate over to low-carb, as most alternatives to croutons won't float to hold the cheese in place. Rather than give up on that French onion flavor, I've simply reinvented by using the same combination of ingredients (minus those pesky croutons) as the basis for this hearty quiche.

SHOPPING LIST

Nonstick cooking spray
2 tablespoons butter
1 large yellow onion, thinly sliced
1/2 cup beef stock
8 ounces sliced provolone cheese
8 large eggs
3/4 cup heavy cream
1/2 teaspoon salt
1/4 teaspoon pepper
1/4 teaspoon dried thyme
1/4 teaspoon onion powder

HELPFUL TIPS

I've listed the ounces for the provolone cheese, rather than the number of slices, as that tends to differ from brand to brand, but any standard package should be 8 ounces.

1. Preheat oven to 350°F. Spray an 8-inch deep dish pie plate with nonstick cooking spray.
2. Heat butter and onions in a skillet over medium heat, stirring infrequently, until onions begin to cook down and caramelize, about 10 minutes.
3. Raise heat to high and stir beef stock into the onions. Bring to a simmer and let cook until nearly all of the stock has evaporated. Quickly remove pan from heat.
4. Transfer onions to the prepared pie plate, spreading across the bottom. Lightly top with overlapping slices of the provolone cheese.
5. In a mixing bowl, whisk together the eggs, heavy cream, salt, pepper, thyme, and onion powder.
6. Pour the egg mixture over the onions and cheese in the pie plate. Tap the pie plate on the counter lightly to let the eggs flow under the cheese.
7. Bake 40 minutes, just until set and slightly springy in the center. Let cool 5 minutes before serving warm.

Calories: 325 • Fat: 26g • Protein: 19g • Total Carbs: 4.5g - Fiber: 0.5g = Net Carbs: 4g

PREP TIME: 15 MIN • COOK TIME: 20 MIN • SERVES: 4

PORTABELLA EGGS BENEDICT

Eggs Benedict can be a pretty complicated recipe to make from scratch, but I've done my best to simplify things here. Serving atop a roasted portabella mushroom cap, rather than an English muffin, keeps the carbs low, while adding even more flavor to the final dish.

SHOPPING LIST

Nonstick cooking spray

4 portabella mushrooms, stems removed

1 tablespoon olive oil

Salt and pepper

4 large eggs

4 slices Canadian bacon

HOLLANDAISE SAUCE

2 large egg yolks

2 teaspoons lemon juice

1/4 cup butter, melted

Pinch salt

HELPFUL TIPS

Making this recipe is all about timing. Because I've ensured that the oven temperature is the same throughout, simply place the eggs in the oven 8 minutes after the mushrooms have gone in and everything will be finished at the same time.

1. Place two oven racks in middle positions and preheat oven to 350°F. Spray a sheet pan and 4 cups of a muffin tin with nonstick cooking spray. Place a sauce pot filled with 3 inches of water over medium heat.
2. Toss mushrooms in olive oil, generously season with salt and pepper, and place on the prepared sheet pan. Bake 20 minutes, or until tender.
3. Meanwhile, add 1 tablespoon of water to each of 4 prepared muffin cups. Crack an egg over the water in each. Bake 12 minutes, just until whites are set, but yolk is still runny. The tops of the eggs will be wet, however, this is just the water that was added to oven-poach them.
4. As eggs are cooking, prepare the Hollandaise Sauce. Ensure the water in the sauce pot has come to a simmer (if not, raise the heat).
5. In a heat-proof bowl that fits over the sauce pot, whisk the egg yolks and lemon juice until they've doubled in volume.
6. Continue to whisk the yolks as you place the bowl over the sauce pot to create a double-boiler. Slowly drizzle in melted butter as you continuously whisk. Whisk until the sauce has thickened and doubled in volume. Remove from heat and season with salt.
7. Top each baked mushroom cap with a slice of Canadian bacon, then an oven-poached egg. Drizzle with a spoonful of hollandaise before serving.

Calories: 285 • Fat: 24g • Protein: 15g • Total Carbs: 2.5g - Fiber: 0.5g = Net Carbs: 2g

PREP TIME: 10 MIN • COOK TIME: 20 MIN • SERVES: 9

BREAKFAST

CHOCOLATE BANANA NUT MUFFINS

The only thing that could make a banana nut muffin better is... Chocolate! It's like a chocolate covered banana, in a muffin, for breakfast—you simply cannot go wrong.

SHOPPING LIST

Nonstick cooking spray

2 cups almond flour

1 cup sugar substitute

1/3 cup chopped walnuts

3 tablespoons unsweetened cocoa powder

2 teaspoons baking powder

4 large eggs

1 large egg white

3 tablespoons butter, melted

2 teaspoons banana extract

HELPFUL TIPS

You can also use paper liners to line the muffin tin; however, you should still spray the insides of the liners with nonstick cooking spray.

1. Place oven rack in the center position and preheat to 350°F. Spray 9 muffin cups with nonstick cooking spray.
2. In a large mixing bowl, combine the almond flour, sugar substitute, walnuts, cocoa powder, and baking powder.
3. In a separate mixing bowl, beat the eggs, egg white, melted butter, and banana extract until frothy.
4. Beat the wet ingredients into the dry ingredients, until all is combined.
5. Fill the 9 prepared muffin cups with an equal amount of the finished batter.
6. Bake for 18–20 minutes, or until centers are firm and springy, and a toothpick inserted into a muffin comes out mostly clean.

Calories: 255 • Fat: 21.5g • Protein: 10g • Total Carbs: 9.5g - Fiber: 3.5g = Net Carbs: 6g

LUNCH

five ingredient recipe

grilling recipe

PREP TIME: 20 MIN • CHILL TIME: 1 HR • SERVES: 4

PULLED PORK PICNIC IN A JAR

I try not to get swept up in the latest food trends, but the jar-craze is hard to avoid. For many people, it's about the practicality of being able to take your lunch to work in one container—but for me, I think it can really make a great presentation, especially for a Southern meal like this coleslaw topped with pulled pork, pickles, and bell pepper. It's also a good use for pulled pork leftovers, which go great in this warm or chilled.

SHOPPING LIST

COLESLAW

1 (16-ounce) bag shredded coleslaw mix

1/3 cup mayonnaise

3 tablespoons sugar substitute

1/3 cup half and half

1 tablespoon cider vinegar

1/2 teaspoon salt

1/4 teaspoon pepper

1/4 teaspoon onion powder

PICNIC JARS

4 empty 16-ounce jars

1/2 batch Carolina Pulled Pork, recipe page 133

1/2 cup sliced dill pickles

1/4 cup diced red bell pepper

1. In a food storage container, combine all coleslaw ingredients, shaking to evenly coat cabbage. Refrigerate at least 1 hour.
2. Fill 2/3 of each empty jar with the coleslaw.
3. Top the coleslaw in each jar with the prepared Carolina Pulled Pork, filling to right below the lip of the jar.
4. Cover the pulled pork in each jar with the pickle slices before sprinkling diced red bell pepper over top all.

HELPFUL TIPS

While the jars make the best presentation, obviously this can be made in individual bowls as well.

Calories: 580 • Fat: 40.5 • Protein: 43.5g • Total Carbs: 7g - Fiber: 1.5g = **Net Carbs: 5.5g**

PREP TIME: 20 MIN • COOK TIME: 25 MIN • SERVES: 4

CHICKEN AND "RICE" SOUP

Grated cauliflower "rice" makes for this easy reinvention of the classic chicken and rice soup. It's a one-pot lunch that makes 4 portions so hearty, you'll be sure to fill up, even without the starch.

SHOPPING LIST

2 tablespoons butter
2 boneless, skinless chicken breasts
1/2 cup diced yellow onion
2 stalks celery, diced
2 carrots, peeled and diced
5 cups chicken stock
2 sprigs fresh thyme
1 bay leaf
1/2 teaspoon salt
1/4 teaspoon pepper
2 cups grated cauliflower (see tips)
1/2 cup heavy cream

HELPFUL TIPS

Cauliflower rice is now available already grated in both the produce section and freezer section of most grocery stores. You can also make your own by grating fresh cauliflower using the large holes of a cheese grater.

1. Heat butter in a pot over medium-high heat.
2. Add chicken, onion, celery, and carrots and cook until chicken begins to brown, about 4 minutes on each side.
3. Add the chicken stock, thyme, bay leaf, salt, and pepper and bring up to a boil.
4. Reduce heat to medium and let simmer 10 minutes.
5. Remove chicken from the pot and let cool as you add the grated cauliflower and heavy cream. Let cook 4 minutes, just until cauliflower rice is tender. Remove from heat.
6. Meanwhile, shred the cooked chicken into bite-sized pieces before adding back into the soup.
7. Remove thyme and bay leaf and adjust the amount of salt and pepper to taste before serving.

Calories: 260 • Fat: 13g • Protein: 28.5g • Total Carbs: 8.5g - Fiber: 2.5g = Net Carbs: 6g

PREP TIME: 20 MIN • COOK TIME: 12 MIN • MAKES: 8 • SERVES: 4

CHEESEBURGER SKEWERS

When you need to ditch that burger's bun, these skewers make for a far better presentation than simply reaching for that fork and knife. Be sure to serve alongside mustard and no-sugar-added ketchup for dipping.

SHOPPING LIST

1 pound lean ground beef

1 large egg

1 teaspoon salt

1/2 teaspoon pepper

1/4 teaspoon onion powder

2 tablespoons vegetable oil

16 pieces cubed Cheddar cheese

8 cherry tomatoes

1 jumbo dill pickle, cut into 8 large chunks

Large bamboo skewers

HELPFUL TIPS

To make these easier, simply buy pre-cut Cheddar cheese cubes.

1. In a large mixing bowl, use your hands to combine ground beef, egg, salt, and pepper.
2. Form the ground beef mixture into 16 tightly-formed meatballs that are a little smaller than a ping pong ball.
3. Heat the vegetable oil in a large skillet over medium-high heat.
4. Place the meatballs in the skillet and brown on all sides, cooking until cooked throughout, about 12 minutes.
5. Thread a cooked meatball onto a bamboo skewer, then a chunk of Cheddar cheese, then a cherry tomato, then a second meatball, a second chunk of Cheddar cheese, and finally a chunk of pickle.
6. Repeat until you've made 8 full skewers. Serve immediately.

Calories: 315 • Fat: 20g • Protein: 31g • Total Carbs: 2.5g - Fiber: 0.5g = Net Carbs: 2g

ZUCCHINI RAMEN BOWL

Spiralized zucchini noodles make for an absolutely spot-on reinvention of ramen, cooking themselves right in the serving bowl thanks to a piping hot (and simple) broth. While I suggest hardboiled egg and carrots, you can top the bowl with any ingredients of your choice, especially leftover pork or chicken.

SHOPPING LIST

2 1/2 cups beef stock or broth

1 tablespoon soy sauce

1 teaspoon rice wine vinegar (see tip)

1/4 teaspoon onion powder

1/8 teaspoon white pepper

1 large zucchini, spiralized into noodles

1 hardboiled egg, halved

1/4 cup matchstick cut carrots

1 teaspoon sesame oil

HELPFUL TIPS

Rice wine vinegar goes best with these flavors, however, ordinary white vinegar can be used in a pinch.

1. Place the beef stock, soy sauce, rice wine vinegar, onion powder, and white pepper in a pot over high heat.
2. Bring the broth up to a boil and let cook 1 minute.
3. Meanwhile arrange the zucchini noodles in a large serving bowl. Top with hardboiled egg and carrots.
4. Pour the boiling hot broth over the ingredients in the bowl.
5. Drizzle with sesame oil before serving.

Calories: 205 • Fat: 9.5g • Protein: 15g • Total Carbs: 12g - Fiber: 4g = Net Carbs: 8g

PREP TIME: 15 MIN • COOK TIME: 20 MIN • SERVES: 4

LOADED "POTATO" SOUP

My Loaded Mock Mashed Potatoes has to be one of the five most popular recipes I've ever created, but this recipe takes that same idea (of using cauliflower in place of high-carb potatoes) from a side dish to a fulfilling full lunch in a bowl. We all know that the toppings are where the flavor is, so be sure to pile them on!

LUNCH

SHOPPING LIST

2 tablespoons butter
1/2 cup diced yellow onion
2 teaspoons minced garlic
1 medium head cauliflower, chopped
4 cups chicken stock
3/4 cup heavy cream
3/4 teaspoon salt
1/2 teaspoon pepper
1/4 teaspoon onion powder
Shredded Cheddar cheese, to top
Crumbled bacon, to top
Chopped fresh chives, to top

HELPFUL TIPS

If you are concerned about transferring the hot soup to a blender, you can let it cool before blending, then return to the stove to reheat before serving.

1. Heat butter, onion, and garlic in a pot over medium-high heat, sautéing 3 minutes, until onions are translucent.
2. Add the cauliflower and sauté 2 minutes.
3. Stir in chicken stock and bring up to a boil. Reduce heat to medium and let simmer 12 minutes, or until cauliflower is very tender.
4. Stir in heavy cream, salt, pepper, and onion powder and bring back to a simmer.
5. Remove from heat and use an immersion blender to completely blend the cauliflower into the broth. You can also do this by transferring in 2 batches to a heat-proof blender or food processor.
6. Serve soup topped with Cheddar cheese, bacon, and chives.

Calories: 175 • Fat: 15g • Protein: 4g • Total Carbs: 9.5g - Fiber: 3g = Net Carbs: 6.5g

PREP TIME: 15 MIN • COOK TIME: 10 MIN • SERVES: 4

GRILLED CHICKEN CAESAR BOATS

This chicken Caesar salad is literally all wrapped up. Large leaves of romaine lettuce make the perfect "boat" to each hold two grilled chicken tenders, tomatoes, dressing, and shredded Parmesan cheese. For even more stability, and to ensure you can eat these with your hands, simply double up on the lettuce leaves, placing two on top of each other to reinforce themselves.

SHOPPING LIST

8 chicken tenderloins (about 1 pound)

1 tablespoon vegetable oil

Salt and pepper

4 large leaves romaine lettuce

8 cherry tomatoes, halved

1/3 cup Caesar salad dressing (see tip)

1/3 cup shredded Parmesan cheese

HELPFUL TIPS

Look for a Caesar salad dressing without added sugars, or create your own by combining 1/2 cup mayonnaise, 1/4 cup grated Parmesan cheese, 1 teaspoon lemon juice, 1/2 teaspoon Worcestershire sauce, 1/2 teaspoon minced garlic and salt and pepper to taste. A teaspoon of anchovy paste will make it even better.

1. Oil and preheat an outdoor grill, indoor grill, or grill pan to high heat.
2. Toss chicken tenderloins in vegetable oil and generously season with salt and pepper.
3. Place on grill perpendicular to the grill's grates to prevent the tenderloins from falling through.
4. Grill for 5 minutes on the first side, then flip and grill an additional 4 minutes, or until a meat thermometer inserted into the thickest piece registers 165°F.
5. Lay out the large leaves of romaine lettuce and place two grilled chicken tenders in each, placing them end to end or slightly overlapping to fill the entire length of the leaves.
6. Top the chicken in each lettuce leaf with 4 halves of tomato.
7. Drizzle the filling in each leaf with Caesar dressing before sprinkling with a generous amount of the shredded Parmesan cheese. Serve warm.

Calories: 225 • Fat: 12g • Protein: 27.5g • Total Carbs: 3g - Fiber: 0.5g = **Net Carbs: 2.5g**

PREP TIME: 20 MIN • CHILL TIME: 1 HR • SERVES: 6

ITALIAN "PASTA" SALAD

While pasta salad is typically made with short macaroni-style shapes, this low-carb re-creation uses long zucchini and yellow squash noodles, as they are truly the best alternative to pasta. Cherry tomatoes, mini mozzarella pearls, and diced salami complete the salad, which is then tossed in a homemade Italian dressing.

SHOPPING LIST

SALAD

2 large zucchini, spiralized into noodles

2 large yellow squash, spiralized into noodles

1 cup cherry tomatoes, halved

8 ounces fresh mozzarella pearls

1/2 cup diced Italian salami

DRESSING

1/4 cup extra-virgin olive oil

3 tablespoons red wine vinegar

2 teaspoons sugar substitute

2 teaspoons Dijon mustard

1 1/2 teaspoons Italian seasoning

1 teaspoon minced garlic

1/2 teaspoon salt

1/4 teaspoon pepper

1. Place all salad ingredients in a large serving bowl or food storage container.
2. In a mixing bowl, whisk together all Dressing ingredients.
3. Pour the dressing over the salad and toss to evenly coat.
4. Cover and refrigerate for 1 hour before serving.

HELPFUL TIPS

If you don't own a spiralizer to cut vegetable noodles, you can also use a vegetable peeler to thinly slice them into long ribbons.

Calories: 275 • Fat: 21.5g • Protein: 12.5g • Total Carbs: 9.5g - Fiber: 3g = Net Carbs: 6.5g

PREP TIME: 30 MIN • COOK TIME: 12 MINS • SERVES: 4

BUFFALO COBB SALAD

No two Cobb Salads are exactly alike, and this one is especially unlike most others! With buffalo sauce on the chicken, and mixed into the blue cheese dressing, you get the heat of the hot sauce and the cooling of the dressing all in one. Sliced celery and green onions are added to the more typical topping of egg and avocado to better complement the buffalo sauce. I usually leave bacon out, as I find that this is enough toppings, but you can add it, if desired.

SHOPPING LIST

1 tablespoon vegetable oil

3 boneless, skinless chicken breasts

Salt and pepper

2 tablespoons Louisiana hot sauce, divided

1 tablespoon butter, melted

1/3 cup blue cheese dressing (see tip)

1 head romaine lettuce, chopped

3 hardboiled eggs, chopped

1 avocado, diced

2/3 cup crumbled blue cheese

3 stalks celery, sliced

3 green onions, sliced

HELPFUL TIPS

We purchase refrigerated blue cheese dressing from the produce section, as those brands tend to be the most natural and lowest in carbs.

1. Heat vegetable oil in a skillet over medium-high heat.
2. Generously season chicken with salt and pepper before adding to the skillet. Cook for 6 minutes on each side, or until a meat thermometer inserted into the thickest piece registers 165°F. Let cool completely.
3. Chop chicken breasts into bite-sized cubes or pieces, then toss in 1 tablespoon of the hot sauce and all of the melted butter.
4. Prepare the dressing by stirring the remaining tablespoon of hot sauce into the prepared blue cheese dressing.
5. Prepare the salad by placing the lettuce into a large salad bowl or 4 individual bowls.
6. Top the large salad or individual salads with rows of each the cooked and coated chicken, hardboiled eggs, avocado, blue cheese, celery, and green onion.
7. Serve with the dressing on the side or drizzled over top.

Calories: 460 • Fat: 31g • Protein: 38g • Total Carbs: 9g - Fiber: 3.5g = **Net Carbs: 5.5g**

PREP TIME: 20 MIN • COOK TIME: 10 MIN • SERVES: 8

CHICAGO-STYLE PICKLE DOGS

Chicago-style hot dogs are typically served topped with a large dill pickle spear, but my version eliminates the high-carb bun by serving the pickle topped with the dog! It's everything you love, presented in a fun and unique way. In my recipe, I've also eliminated the traditional slices of tomato to make these easier to eat, but you can feel free to add them if you don't mind getting messy.

SHOPPING LIST

8 bun-length all-natural hot dogs

8 whole jumbo dill pickles, room temperature

Sugar substitute, optional

1/2 cup finely diced white onion

Yellow mustard

Celery seed or celery salt (see tip)

HELPFUL TIPS

I suggest whole celery seed to top these dogs, as they do not need the additional salt contained in celery salt, however, the celery salt can be used, if desired.

1. Place hot dogs in a skillet and fill with 1 inch of water. Cover and cook over medium-high heat.
2. Bring the water in the skillet to a simmer and let hot dogs cook until hot throughout, about 5 minutes. For a bit of color on the dogs (not traditional in a Chicago-style dog) drain water and sauté over medium-high heat until they've reached your desired browning.
3. Meanwhile, slice the pickles lengthwise 4/5 of the way through the entire pickle, allowing you to open them like a hot dog bun.
4. If desired, lightly sprinkle the inside of each pickle with about 1/4 teaspoon of sugar substitute to add a touch of sweetness. This will mimic the sweet relish that usually tops a Chicago-style dog.
5. Place a cooked hot dog into each pickle bun and top with diced onion, yellow mustard, and a sprinkling of celery seed. Serve with napkins!

Calories: 145 • Fat: 12.5g • Protein: 5g • Total Carbs: 5g - Fiber: 4g = **Net Carbs: 1g**

PREP TIME: 15 MIN • COOK TIME: 30 MIN • SERVES: 4

ROASTED TOMATO AND CHEDDAR SOUP

Roasting fresh Roma tomatoes at a high heat brings a ton of flavor to this creamy soup. Cheddar cheese is mixed right into the soup, giving you the classic combination of a grilled cheese with tomato soup, all in the same bowl!

SHOPPING LIST

Nonstick cooking spray

8 medium Roma tomatoes, chopped

1 tablespoon olive oil

1 tablespoon butter

1/4 cup minced yellow onion

2 teaspoons minced garlic

3 cups chicken stock or broth

2 tablespoons tomato paste

2 sprigs fresh thyme

1/2 teaspoon salt

1/4 teaspoon pepper

3/4 cup heavy cream

1 cup shredded sharp Cheddar cheese

HELPFUL TIPS

This is great when served alongside my Cloud Bread, recipe page 147.

1. Preheat oven to 400°F. Line a sheet pan with aluminum foil and spray with nonstick cooking spray.
2. Toss the chopped tomatoes in olive oil and spread out on the prepared sheet pan.
3. Bake 20 minutes, until tomatoes begin to wilt.
4. Meanwhile, heat butter, onion, and garlic in a pot over medium-high heat, sautéing 5 minutes, until onions begin to lightly caramelize.
5. Add the roasted tomatoes and chicken stock to a blender or food processor and blend until smooth.
6. Pour the blended tomatoes into the pot with the onions and garlic, then add the tomato paste, thyme, salt, and pepper. Bring to a simmer and reduce heat to medium.
7. Stir in the heavy cream, bring back to a simmer, then reduce heat to low. Let simmer over low heat for 5 minutes.
8. Remove from heat and slowly stir in Cheddar cheese before removing thyme to serve.

Calories: 280 • Fat: 24g • Protein: 9.5g • Total Carbs: 9.5g - Fiber: 2g = Net Carbs: 7.5g

PREP TIME: 20 MIN • CHILL TIME: 2 HRS • SERVES: 6

THAI PEANUT SLAW

This is anything but your typical coleslaw! With green onions, fresh cilantro, and roasted peanuts and a dressing made with peanut butter, soy sauce, and rice wine vinegar—this slaw packs classic Thai flavors into a salad that goes great alongside any Asian dish. It's even great when served warm.

SHOPPING LIST

DRESSING

1/4 cup all-natural peanut butter

2 tablespoons half and half

2 tablespoons sugar substitute

1 1/2 tablespoons rice wine vinegar

1 tablespoon soy sauce

2 teaspoons sesame oil

1 1/2 teaspoons minced garlic

1/2 teaspoon crushed red pepper flakes

SLAW

1 (16-ounce) bag shredded coleslaw mix

1/2 cup roasted peanuts

1/3 cup sliced green onions

1/4 cup chopped cilantro

1. Place all Dressing ingredients in a large food storage container and whisk to combine.
2. Add the Slaw ingredients to the dressing, cover, and shake to coat the vegetables.
3. Refrigerate at least 2 hours before serving chilled or gently warmed in the microwave in 30-second intervals.

HELPFUL TIPS

You may want to adjust the final slaw to taste by adding additional rice wine vinegar, soy sauce, and/or sugar substitute to get that perfect balance of acid, salt, and sweet.

Calories: 140 • Fat: 11g • Protein: 5.5g • Total Carbs: 7g - Fiber: 3g = **Net Carbs: 4g**

PREP TIME: 10 MIN • COOK TIME: 5 MIN • CHILL TIME: 1 HR • SERVES: 4

GRILLED ASPARAGUS SALAD

This is a simple but impressive salad made with only a few non-pantry ingredients. While you can use steamed asparagus (see my tips below) rather than grilled, grilling the asparagus really makes the final salad stand out, both in flavor and presentation.

SHOPPING LIST

1 pound asparagus, stalks trimmed by 1 1/2 inches

3 tablespoons olive oil, divided

Salt and pepper

1 cup cherry tomatoes, halved

Juice of 1/2 lemon

1 1/2 teaspoons minced garlic

Pinch sugar substitute, optional

1/2 cup shaved Parmesan cheese

HELPFUL TIPS

You can also make this with lightly steamed asparagus, rather than grilled. It's best when the asparagus are still a bit crisp after cooking, so only steam for 2–3 minutes.

1. Oil and preheat an outdoor grill, indoor grill, or grill pan to high heat.
2. Toss asparagus in 2 tablespoons of the olive oil and generously season with salt and pepper.
3. Place on grill perpendicular to the grill's grates to prevent the asparagus from falling through, or use a grilling basket to ensure that they cannot.
4. Grill for 4 minutes, flipping halfway through. Remove from grill and let cool 10 minutes.
5. Toss asparagus with tomatoes, lemon juice, garlic, sugar substitute, and the remaining tablespoon of olive oil. Season lightly with salt and pepper.
6. Cover and refrigerate for 1 hour before serving topped with the shaved Parmesan cheese.

Calories: 140 • Fat: 11.5g • Protein: 4g • Total Carbs: 7g - Fiber: 3g = Net Carbs: 4g

STARTERS

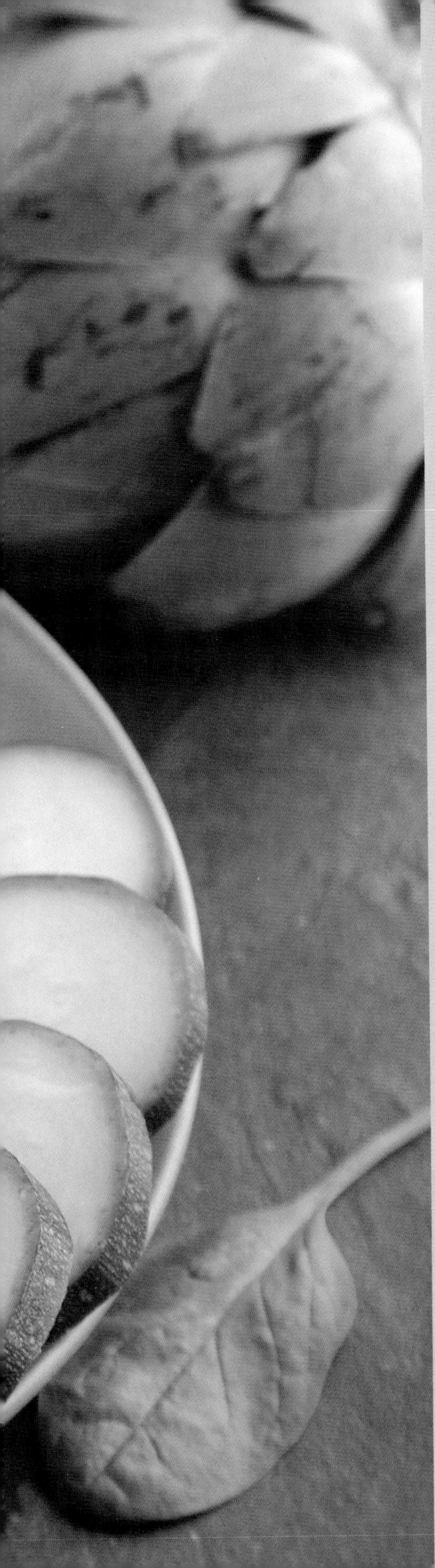

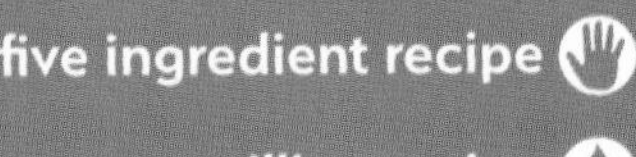
five ingredient recipe
grilling recipe

PREP TIME: 10 MIN • COOK TIME: 55 MIN • SERVES: 8

CHIPOTLE CHICKEN WINGS

These wings bring the smoky heat of chipotle in a quick and easy dry rub made using only a few simple ingredients. It's an entirely new take on "hot wings" that makes a perfect appetizer or party food, especially on those big game days.

SHOPPING LIST

3 pounds fresh chicken wings, drum and wing separated

2 tablespoons olive oil

Juice of 1/2 lime

2 tablespoons ground chipotle

1 teaspoon onion powder

3/4 teaspoon salt

1/2 teaspoon ground cumin

1/2 teaspoon pepper

1. Preheat oven to 375°F. Line a sheet pan with aluminum foil.
2. In a large mixing bowl, toss wings in all other ingredients to fully coat.
3. Spread the wings out onto the prepared sheet pan, arranging in a single layer.
4. Bake for 50–55 minutes, or until slicing into the thickest drum reveals no pink. Serve immediately.

HELPFUL TIPS

Frozen chicken wings can be used in this recipe as long as they are fully thawed in the refrigerator before cooking. For a bit of sweetness to offset the heat of the chipotle, add 2 teaspoons of sugar substitute to the rub before baking.

Calories: 365 • Fat: 29g • Protein: 25.5g • Total Carbs: 0.5g - Fiber: 0g = Net Carbs: 0.5g

PREP TIME: 15 MIN • COOK TIME: 15 MIN • SERVES: 8

SPINACH AND ARTICHOKE DIP

What I love about Spinach and Artichoke Dip is that it is delicious when fresh made and hot, but just as good when the leftovers are served chilled the next day! My favorite dipper is sliced zucchini, as they're firm enough to grab whole chunks of artichoke.

STARTERS

SHOPPING LIST

1 tablespoon olive oil

1/2 cup diced yellow onion

1 tablespoon minced garlic

10 ounces frozen chopped spinach

8 ounces cream cheese

1 cup sour cream

1/3 cup mayonnaise

1 cup grated Parmesan cheese

1 teaspoon Worcestershire sauce

1/4 teaspoon onion powder

1/4 teaspoon pepper

1 (14-ounce) can artichoke hearts, drained and chopped

Salt to taste

HELPFUL TIPS

If the dip overly thickens, simply thin it out with a little half and half, or even water.

1. Heat the olive oil in a sauce pot over medium heat.
2. Add the onion and garlic and sauté 3 minutes, just until onions are translucent.
3. Add the chopped spinach; cover, and cook, stirring occasionally, until fully defrosted.
4. Reduce heat to low and add the cream cheese, sour cream, mayonnaise, Parmesan cheese, Worcestershire sauce, onion powder, and pepper.
5. Alternate between covering the dip and stirring to keep the cheese from burning, just until dip is bubbly hot.
6. Stir in artichoke hearts and season with salt to taste before serving warm or chilled.

Calories: 315 • Fat: 29g • Protein: 10.5g • Total Carbs: 6g - Fiber: 1.5g = **Net Carbs: 4.5g**

PREP TIME: 20 MIN • COOK TIME: 20 MIN • MAKES: 18 • SERVES: 6

ARUGULA PESTO PARTY MEATBALLS

Basil isn't the only green that makes for a great pesto sauce. In this recipe, I use peppery arugula to make the pesto, and then stir half of the sauce directly into the meatballs to bake the flavor throughout. Rather than blend pine nuts into the sauce, I leave them whole to add texture to the meatballs.

SHOPPING LIST

Nonstick cooking spray

ARUGULA PESTO

2 cups arugula

1/2 cup grated Parmesan cheese

1/3 cup extra-virgin olive oil

2 cloves garlic

MEATBALLS

1 pound lean ground beef

1 large egg, beaten

1/4 cup toasted pine nuts (see tip)

1/2 teaspoon salt

1/4 teaspoon pepper

1. Preheat oven to 375°F. Spray a sheet pan with nonstick cooking spray.
2. Prepare the Arugula Pesto by adding all ingredients to a food processor and processing until smooth.
3. Place 1/2 of the prepared Arugula Pesto in a large mixing bowl and add all Meatballs ingredients.
4. Using your hands, combine all of the ingredients in the bowl and form into 18 equal-sized meatballs. Transfer to the prepared sheet pan.
5. Bake 20 minutes, or until slicing into the largest meatballs reveals no pink.
6. Toss baked meatballs in the remaining 1/2 of the Arugula Pesto before serving with toothpicks alongside.

HELPFUL TIPS

The easiest way to evenly toast the pine nuts is to bake at 375°F for 5–7 minutes, just until lightly browned.

Calories: 330 • Fat: 23.5g • Protein: 29g • Total Carbs: 1.5g - Fiber: 0.5g = **Net Carbs: 1g**

PREP TIME: 20 MIN • COOK TIME: 15 MIN • MAKES: 16 • SERVES: 4

CLASSIC STUFFED MUSHROOMS

Stuffed mushrooms make for a perfect low-carb appetizer, as long as you stuff them with the right ingredients. I've done a lot of variations on them over the years, usually stuffing them with cream cheese or meat, but I've never taken a stab at a traditional, breadcrumb-stuffed mushroom until now. The low-carb "breadcrumbs" in this recipe are packed with flavor and bake up soft and silky smooth, almost like cornmeal stuffing.

SHOPPING LIST

Nonstick cooking spray

1 pound large button mushrooms (about 16 mushrooms)

Salt

2 teaspoons vegetable oil

1/4 cup almond flour

2 tablespoons grated Parmesan cheese

1 tablespoon minced red onion

1 tablespoon butter, melted

2 large leaves fresh sage, minced

1/2 teaspoon lemon juice

1/4 teaspoon dried thyme

1/4 teaspoon pepper

HELPFUL TIPS

For even more browning on the filling, you can place these under the broiler for 2 minutes after baking.

1. Preheat oven to 375°F. Spray a sheet pan with nonstick cooking spray.
2. Scrub mushrooms clean. Remove stems and discard 1/2 of the stems. Lightly sprinkle the insides of the mushrooms with salt to season.
3. Place vegetable oil in a skillet over medium-high heat. Mince the remaining 1/2 of the mushroom stems and add to the skillet, cooking until softened. Drain all excess liquid and transfer the cooked stems to a small mixing bowl.
4. Add all remaining ingredients to the cooked stems and whisk with a fork to create a dry and crumbly filling.
5. Stuff each mushroom until overflowing with the filling.
6. Place the stuffed mushrooms on the prepared sheet pan.
7. Bake 15 minutes, or until mushrooms are tender and filling is beginning to brown. Let cool 5 minutes before serving.

Calories: 130 • Fat: 10g • Protein: 7g • Total Carbs: 6g - Fiber: 2g = Net Carbs: 4g

PREP TIME: 20 MIN • COOK TIME: 8 MIN • MAKES: 12 • SERVES: 6

CAPRESE SWEET PEPPER POPPERS

Mozzarella cheese and fresh basil are stuffed into miniature sweet peppers to make these colorful (and flavorful) party poppers. They're super simple to make, but are sure to make a real impact when served to guests.

SHOPPING LIST

12 mini sweet peppers

4 mozzarella string cheese sticks

12 leaves fresh basil

1 tablespoon olive oil

Salt

1 tablespoon balsamic vinegar

HELPFUL TIPS

These are also extremely good when stuffed with Cheddar cheese sticks wrapped in 1/2 slice of cooked bacon.

1 Place oven rack in top position and preheat broiler to high heat. Line a sheet pan with aluminum foil.

2 Leaving the green tops of the peppers intact, slice a slit down the length of the pepper. Scoop out any seeds and discard.

3 Slice each cheese stick into three 2-inch pieces. Wrap each piece in a basil leaf and then stuff into a sliced pepper.

4 Place the stuffed peppers on the prepared sheet pan, cut-side up. Drizzle all with olive oil and flip to coat before seasoning with salt.

5 Broil for 6–8 minutes, just until peppers begin to char. Drizzle with balsamic vinegar before serving.

Calories: 100 • Fat: 5.5g • Protein: 6g • Total Carbs: 6g - Fiber: 2g = Net Carbs: 4g

PREP TIME: 10 MIN • COOK TIME: 5 MIN • MAKES: 6 • SERVES: 6

ALBACORE TUNA CAKES

These tuna cakes make an inexpensive alternative to crab cakes you can whip up using mostly pantry staples you're likely to already have on hand. Even the chopped chives can be substituted with 1/2 teaspoon of onion powder in a pinch.

SHOPPING LIST

1 (5-ounce) can albacore tuna, drained

1 large egg, beaten

2 tablespoons mayonnaise

2 tablespoons milled flax seed

1 tablespoon chopped chives

1 teaspoon Dijon mustard

1 1/2 teaspoons baking powder

1 1/2 teaspoons Old Bay seasoning

2 tablespoons vegetable oil

HELPFUL TIPS

For more color, add 2 tablespoons of diced red bell pepper or roasted red peppers to the batter before cooking.

1 In a mixing bowl, fold together all ingredients, except vegetable oil, to create the tuna cake batter.

2 Heat the vegetable oil in a large skillet or griddle over medium-high heat.

3 Spoon 6 rounded tablespoons of the batter into the hot skillet and lightly press down to flatten.

4 Cook until lightly browned, about 2–3 minutes on each side. Serve hot.

Calories: 115 • Fat: 10g • Protein: 6g • Total Carbs: 1.5g - Fiber: 0.5g = **Net Carbs: 1g**

PREP TIME: 10 MIN • CHILL TIME: 2 HRS • SERVES: 8

MARINATED CREAM CHEESE SPREAD

This simple recipe makes for an easy alternative to store-bought cheese logs, which contain too many ingredients to count, including added sugar. A whole brick of cream cheese is marinated and topped with olives and oregano, making a flavorful spread to serve alongside sliced zucchini or cucumbers.

STARTERS

SHOPPING LIST

1 (8-ounce) brick cream cheese, cold

1/4 cup pitted Kalamata olives

3 tablespoons extra-virgin olive oil

1 tablespoon white wine vinegar

1 teaspoon minced garlic

1 teaspoon dried oregano

1/4 teaspoon pepper

HELPFUL TIPS

For even more flavor, add 2 tablespoons of roasted red peppers or diced pimentos to the olive marinade before food processing.

1. Place cold brick of cream cheese on a serving platter, leaving the shape intact.
2. Add all remaining ingredients to a food processor and pulse until olives are minced.
3. Spread the olive marinade over the top of the brick of cream cheese.
4. Cover and refrigerate at least 2 hours before serving. Refrigerating overnight is best.

Calories: 150 • Fat: 16g • Protein: 2g • Total Carbs: 1g - Fiber: 0g = Net Carbs: 1g

PREP TIME: 30 MIN • COOK TIME: 7 MIN • MAKES: 8 • SERVES: 8

PESTO CHICKEN SKEWERS

Whether you serve these as a grab-and-go appetizer, or serve multiple skewers as an entrée, the bright flavor of fresh pesto is sure to *stick* with you.

SHOPPING LIST

Bamboo skewers

1 pound boneless, skinless chicken breasts

2 yellow squash

1 large zucchini

1 pound small button mushrooms

PESTO SAUCE

2 cups fresh basil leaves

1/2 cup grated Parmesan cheese

1/3 cup extra-virgin olive oil

1/4 cup pine nuts

2 cloves garlic

HELPFUL TIPS

The Pesto Sauce made in this recipe is a great cooking staple that can be made and used for any recipe that you'd like.

1. To prevent charring, soak the bamboo skewers in water for 1 hour before preparing.
2. Cut the chicken breasts into 1 1/4-inch thick cubes, then cut the squash and zucchini into 1-inch thick half circles.
3. Thread a cube of chicken onto the soaked skewer, then a piece of squash, then a mushroom, then finally a piece of zucchini. Repeat to thread a second set of ingredients onto each skewer.
4. Repeat the above step to make 8–10 skewers, as many as your ingredients will allow.
5. Prepare the Pesto Sauce by adding all ingredients to a food processor and processing until smooth.
6. Oil and preheat a conventional grill, indoor grill, or grill pan over high heat.
7. Brush 1/2 of the Pesto Sauce over the skewers.
8. Place the skewers on the grill and cook for 4 minutes on the first side, then flip and cook an additional 3 minutes on the opposite side.
9. Remove from grill and use a clean brush to brush the cooked skewers with the remaining pesto sauce before serving.

Calories: 185 • Fat: 11g • Protein: 20g • Total Carbs: 5g - Fiber: 1.5g = Net Carbs: 3.5g

PREP TIME: 15 MIN • COOK TIME: 7 MIN • SERVES: 6

GRILLED GUACAMOLE

Grilling the avocado before preparing this guacamole adds an entirely new dimension to the flavor, while keeping the ingredients simple and fresh. For the perfect dipper, serve alongside my "Multigrain" Tortilla Chips, recipe page 175.

SHOPPING LIST

3 Hass avocados

2 tablespoons olive oil

1/4 cup chopped cilantro

1/4 cup diced red onion

Juice of 1/2 lime

1 1/2 teaspoons minced garlic

Salt and pepper

HELPFUL TIPS

This works best with avocados that are just on the verge of being ripe and still a tiny bit firm to the squeeze.

1. Oil and preheat a conventional grill, indoor grill, or grill pan over high heat.
2. Cut each avocado in half and remove pits, but do not peel. Toss in olive oil until well coated.
3. Place on grill, cut-side down, cover, and grill 5–7 minutes, or until well-marked.
4. Let cool enough to handle the avocados before using a spoon to scoop the meat out of the peel and into a mixing bowl.
5. Add all remaining ingredients and mash until combined. Season to taste with salt and pepper. Serve warm or chilled.

Calories: 170 • Fat: 16g • Protein: 2.5g • Total Carbs: 8g - Fiber: 5g = Net Carbs: 3g

PREP TIME: 20 MIN • COOK TIME: 20 MIN • SERVES: 6

PIZZERIA CHEESY BREADSTICKS

This low-carb reinvention of the cheesy breadsticks you'd get at a chain pizzeria is just the thing to bust those cravings for both pizza and bread. The secret is in the garlic, roasting over top of these, as that is where you'll get most of that authentic pizzeria flavor.

SHOPPING LIST

1 head cauliflower, roughly chopped

2 large eggs, beaten

1/2 cup grated Parmesan cheese

1 teaspoon Italian seasoning

1/4 teaspoon garlic powder

1/4 teaspoon salt

1/4 teaspoon pepper

2 cups shredded mozzarella cheese, divided

2 teaspoons minced garlic in oil

1 tablespoon chopped fresh parsley

Pizza sauce, for dipping

HELPFUL TIPS

Jarred garlic in oil is best for topping this, as it has a more mild flavor and is less prone to burning at the high oven temperature.

1. Preheat oven to 425°F. Line a sheet pan with parchment paper.
2. Add cauliflower to a food processor and process until very finely grated, almost puréed. Pat with paper towels to remove any excess water.
3. In a mixing bowl, combine grated cauliflower with eggs, Parmesan, Italian seasoning, garlic powder, salt, pepper, and 1 cup of the mozzarella cheese. Fold together until a dough has formed.
4. Place dough on prepared sheet pan, cover with plastic wrap, and roll out until 1/4-inch thick. Discard plastic wrap.
5. Bake 12 minutes. Top with the remaining cup of mozzarella cheese and then sprinkle with the minced garlic.
6. Bake an additional 10 minutes, until cheese begins to brown.
7. Let cool 10 minutes before topping with parsley and slicing into long strips.

Calories: 185 • Fat: 11.5g • Protein: 16g • Total Carbs: 5.5g - Fiber: 1.5g = Net Carbs: 4g

PREP TIME: 30 MIN • MAKES: 24 HALVES • SERVES: 12

DEVILED HAM DEVILED EGGS

Deviled Eggs meet Deviled Ham in this unique take on a potluck favorite. Using dill pickle and a touch of sugar substitute helps replicate sweet relish, without the carbs. That said, 3 tablespoons of no-sugar-added sweet relish can be used in place of both ingredients.

SHOPPING LIST

12 extra large hardboiled eggs, peeled

8 ounces smoked boneless ham steak

1/2 cup mayonnaise

1/2 small dill pickle (or 3 tablespoons minced)

2 tablespoons whole grain mustard

1 tablespoon sugar substitute

Salt and pepper

HELPFUL TIPS

To boil extra-large eggs: Place in a pot and cover with cold water. Bring up to a boil, cover, and remove from heat. Let sit, covered for 15 minutes. Transfer to ice water to stop the cooking process and cool down to prepare the recipe.

1. Cut eggs in half lengthwise and remove yolks. Transfer the egg whites to a serving platter. Transfer the yolks to a food processor.
2. Add ham, mayonnaise, pickle, mustard, and sugar substitute to the food processor and pulse until finely minced and combined, but not entirely smooth. If the mixture is too thick, thin it out with a tablespoon of half and half or water.
3. Season the filling to taste with salt and pepper before spooning into the whites of the eggs. This is made easier with a food storage bag with a large cut made in the corner to pipe the filling into the eggs. Serve cold.

Calories: 175 • Fat: 13.5g • Protein: 11g • Total Carbs: 1.5g - Fiber: 0g = Net Carbs: 1.5g

POULTRY

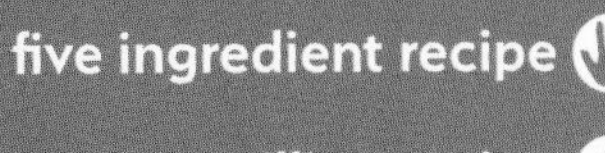
five ingredient recipe
grilling recipe

PREP TIME: 45 MIN • BAKE TIME: 30 MIN • SERVES: 6

CHICKEN POT PIE

In all my time on low-carb I've never attempted a true Chicken Pot Pie with a crust until now. Though it may look complicated, it's a lot easier than you'd think, especially if you start with a store-bought rotisserie chicken for the cooked meat.

SHOPPING LIST

Nonstick cooking spray

TOP CRUST

1 cup almond flour

3/4 cup shredded mozzarella cheese

1 large egg

1/4 teaspoon salt

FILLING

2 tablespoons butter

2 medium yellow squash, chopped

1/2 cup sliced celery

1/2 cup diced yellow onion

1/4 cup diced red bell pepper

1 teaspoon minced garlic

2 cups cooked and chopped chicken

SAUCE

1 (10-ounce) bag frozen cauliflower, thawed

1 1/2 cups chicken stock

1/2 cup heavy cream

1/4 cup grated Parmesan cheese

1/2 teaspoon dried thyme

1/4 teaspoon salt

1/4 teaspoon pepper

1. Spray a 10-inch deep dish pie plate with nonstick cooking spray.
2. Create the Top Crust by placing all Top Crust ingredients to a food processor and processing into a well-combined dough.
3. Roll out the dough over parchment paper until it is the size of your pie plate. Place the plate over the dough and cut around it to trim to a perfect circle. Transfer the trimmed Top Crust to the freezer for 10 minutes.
4. Preheat oven to 400°F.
5. Start the Filling by placing all Filling ingredients in a large skillet over medium-high heat and sautéing for 4 minutes, just until onion is translucent. Drain excess liquid.
6. Place all Sauce ingredients in a food processor and process until entirely smooth. Stir into the ingredients in the skillet and then transfer all to the prepared pie plate.
7. Place the chilled Top Crust over the pie plate and press down over ingredients. Poke 3 holes to vent. If pie crust overlaps the pie plate itself, (as seen in the picture) wrap the edges in aluminum foil to prevent burning. If the crust is only over the filling, this will not be an issue.
8. Bake 25–30 minutes, just until crust is golden brown. Let cool at least 5 minutes before serving.

Calories: 350 • Fat: 25.5g • Protein: 21g • Total Carbs: 11g - Fiber: 4.5g = Net Carbs: 6.5g

PREP TIME: 10 MIN • COOK TIME: 35 MIN • SERVES: 6

CRANBERRY TURKEY TENDERLOIN

This recipe makes a perfect, and quick, holiday entrée for a small family where cooking an entire turkey just isn't necessary. We like to buy fresh cranberries in the winter and freeze them so that we can also prepare this all year round.

SHOPPING LIST

Nonstick cooking spray

1 1/2 pounds turkey tenderloin (may be 2 pieces)

2 tablespoons vegetable oil, divided

Salt and pepper

1 tablespoon chopped fresh sage

1/4 teaspoon ground allspice

1/4 cup diced yellow onion

8 ounces fresh cranberries

3/4 cup water

3/4 cup sugar substitute

1 tablespoon Dijon mustard

Baking soda (see tip)

HELPFUL TIPS

Adding baking soda can cut the tart acidity of the cranberries. If the sauce is too tart for your liking, stir baking soda into the pot, 1/4 teaspoon at a time, until it is to your liking. The sauce will bubble up green, but don't worry, that is just the baking soda neutralizing the acid of the berries. It will dissipate as you stir it in and the final sauce will be a light shade of purple.

1. Preheat oven to 400°F. Spray a deep baking dish, just large enough to fit the tenderloins, with nonstick cooking spray.
2. Place tenderloins into the prepared baking dish and drizzle with 1 tablespoon of the vegetable oil, then season with sage, allspice, and a generous amount of salt and pepper.
3. Bake, uncovered, 25 minutes.
4. Meanwhile, add the remaining tablespoon of oil to a sauce pot over medium-high heat. Add the onions and sauté for 3 minutes, just until translucent.
5. Add the cranberries, water, sugar substitute, and Dijon to the pot and stir to combine.
6. Reduce heat to medium, and let simmer, stirring occasionally, for 15 minutes. Cranberries should have cooked down, into a sauce. Remove from heat and add baking soda to taste to reduce acidity (see tip).
7. Pour over the baked turkey tenderloins and return to the oven, baking an additional 5–10 minutes, until a thermometer inserted into the thickest part of the meat registers 165°F. Let rest 10 minutes before carving to serve topped with cranberry sauce from the baking dish.

Calories: 200 • Fat: 5g • Protein: 28.5g • Total Carbs: 7g - Fiber: 1.5g = Net Carbs: 5.5g

PREP TIME: 5 MIN • CHILL TIME: 1 HR • COOK TIME: 35 MIN • SERVES: 4

CHICKEN UNDER A BRICK

Cooking a whole, split chicken under heavy bricks (you can also use a cast-iron skillet) is the closest you can get to a high-temperature brick oven you'd find in a nice restaurant. It not only allows you to get extra-crispy skin, it's just about the only way to grill a whole chicken, especially with even charring.

SHOPPING LIST

1 whole (3–4-pound) chicken, split to lay flat

1 tablespoon olive oil

Juice of 1/2 lemon

1 tablespoon minced garlic

2 teaspoons chopped fresh rosemary

3/4 teaspoon salt

1/2 teaspoon pepper

HELPFUL TIPS

Splitting a whole bone-in chicken is a bit dangerous for me to recommend, however, you can ask your store's butcher to do this for you.

1. Rub chicken with all other ingredients. For best flavor, cover and refrigerate for 1 hour.
2. Wrap 2 bricks with aluminum foil, or grab a large iron skillet to use in their place. Grilling gloves are also recommended to handle the hot bricks.
3. Oil an outdoor grill (this recipe is not recommended for indoor grills or grill pans). Place the bricks or skillet on grill, cover, and preheat. It is most convenient to place them off to the side, so that you can later place the chicken on the grill without having to move them.
4. Place the chicken on the preheated grill, skin-side down. Using grilling gloves, top chicken with the bricks or skillet and press down. Cover and let cook 15 minutes.
5. Carefully remove bricks and flip chicken. Replace the bricks, cover, and cook 20 additional minutes, or until a meat thermometer inserted into the thickest part of the breast registers 165°F.
6. Let rest 10 minutes before carving.

Calories: 550 • Fat: 40g • Protein: 45g • Total Carbs: 1g - Fiber: 0g = Net Carbs: 1g

PREP TIME: 15 MIN • COOK TIME: 15 MIN • SERVES: 4

CREAMY DIJON CHICKEN SKILLET

This one-skillet meal with chicken and green beans makes feeding the whole family a breeze. Heavy cream and a touch of sugar substitute help to balance out the heat from the Dijon mustard, making for a creamy dish with all bark and no bite.

SHOPPING LIST

2 tablespoons butter

1 pound boneless, skinless chicken breasts, cut into 1-inch cubes

Salt and pepper

1/3 cup diced yellow onion

1/4 cup diced red bell pepper

1 teaspoon minced garlic

1/2 teaspoon dried thyme

1 (12-ounce) bag frozen green beans

2 tablespoons water

1/4 cup heavy cream

1 tablespoon Dijon mustard

1 teaspoon sugar substitute

1. Heat butter in a large skillet over medium-high heat, until sizzling.
2. Generously season cubed chicken with salt and pepper. Add to the hot skillet and cook, stirring occasionally, until browned on all sides, about 5 minutes.
3. Add onion, bell pepper, garlic, and thyme to the skillet and sauté an additional two minutes.
4. Add green beans and water to the skillet, reduce heat to medium, cover, and let cook 5 minutes, or until green beans are heated through.
5. Stir in heavy cream, mustard, and sugar substitute and cook 1 additional minute before serving.

HELPFUL TIPS

Fresh green beans can also be used in this if they are steamed until crisp-tender before adding to the dish.

POULTRY

Calories: 220 • Fat: 10g • Protein: 27.5g • Total Carbs: 6g - Fiber: 2g = Net Carbs: 4g

PREP TIME: 15 MIN • COOK TIME: 15 MIN • SERVES: 6

KANSAS CITY GRILLED CHICKEN BREASTS

In my family, you can't have a casual family cookout without barbecue chicken on the grill. Bone-in chicken breasts can be hard to manage, as the sauce can overly-char before the meat is cooked through. This recipe uses boneless, skinless chicken breasts to overcome that problem and keep you outside by the grill, rather than moving from the grill to the oven.

SHOPPING LIST

6 boneless, skinless chicken breasts

BARBECUE SAUCE

1 (8-ounce) can tomato sauce

1/4 cup sugar substitute

1 1/2 tablespoons cider vinegar

1 1/2 teaspoons liquid smoke

1 teaspoon Worcestershire sauce

1 1/2 teaspoons minced garlic

1 teaspoon smoked paprika

3/4 teaspoon onion powder

3/4 teaspoon salt

1/2 teaspoon black pepper

Pinch ground cloves

HELPFUL TIPS

These can also be baked at 450°F for 15 minutes before tossing in the remaining sauce. Then bake an additional 3 minutes, or until a meat thermometer registers 165°F.

1. In a mixing bowl, combine all Barbecue Sauce ingredients. Transfer 1/2 of the sauce to a separate container and reserve.
2. Toss chicken breasts in the other 1/2 of the sauce and let marinate as you preheat the grill.
3. Oil and preheat an outdoor grill, indoor grill, or grill pan over high heat.
4. Flip chicken breasts to coat in the sauce before placing on the grill. Grill 6 minutes on each side.
5. Quickly toss chicken breasts in the remaining 1/2 of the Barbecue Sauce and return to the grill for just 1 minute longer, or until a meat thermometer inserted into the thickest piece registers 165°F.

Calories: 185 • Fat: 1.5g • Protein: 40g • Total Carbs: 4g - Fiber: 0.5g = Net Carbs: 3.5g

PREP TIME: 15 MIN • COOK TIME: 35 MIN • SERVES: 4

BACON-WRAPPED CHICKEN THIGHS

These simple roasted chicken thighs are seasoned with smoked paprika before being wrapped in smoky bacon. They go straight into the oven with no need to brown them beforehand, saving on time and dishes.

SHOPPING LIST

8 chicken thighs, skin on
1 1/2 teaspoons smoked paprika
1/2 teaspoon salt
1/4 teaspoon pepper
1/4 teaspoon onion powder
1/4 teaspoon garlic powder
8 slices bacon

HELPFUL TIPS

All chicken is at a safe temperature when it reaches 165°F, however, most people prefer the texture of dark meat at around 175°F, so do not be afraid of overcooking.

1. Preheat oven to 375°F.
2. Generously season chicken thighs with smoked paprika, salt, pepper, onion powder, and garlic powder.
3. Stretch bacon to lengthen each strip, then wrap one slice around each seasoned chicken thigh, placing the wrapped thigh skin-side down on a sheet pan.
4. Bake 25 minutes.
5. Flip each chicken thigh and bake 10 additional minutes, or until a meat thermometer inserted into the thickest piece registers 165°F.

Calories: 590 • Fat: 41g • Protein: 53g • Total Carbs: 1g - Fiber: 0g = **Net Carbs: 1g**

PREP TIME: 45 MIN • BAKE TIME: 50 MIN • SERVES: 12

GROUND TURKEY AND EGGPLANT LASAGNA

This low-carb lasagna has thinly sliced eggplant in place of noodles and meat sauce layers made with ground turkey. I like to use Italian-seasoned ground turkey, which tastes like Italian sausage, but regular ground turkey will work just fine as well.

SHOPPING LIST

Nonstick cooking spray

2 large eggplant, thinly sliced

1 tablespoon olive oil

2 pounds Italian seasoned ground turkey

1 cup diced celery

1/2 cup diced yellow onion

2 teaspoons minced garlic

1 (14.5-ounce can) tomato sauce

2 tablespoons tomato paste

1/2 teaspoon salt

1/2 teaspoon pepper

CHEESE FILLING

4 cups shredded mozzarella cheese, divided

16 ounces ricotta cheese

1/2 cup grated Parmesan cheese

1 large egg, beaten

1 teaspoon Italian seasoning

1 teaspoon garlic powder

1/4 teaspoon pepper

1. Preheat oven to 350°F. Spray a 13x9-inch baking dish with nonstick cooking spray.
2. Line a baking sheet with paper towels. Arrange sliced eggplant over top and lightly season both sides with salt to help drain water from the eggplant. Cover with another layer of paper towels and let sit 20 minutes before patting dry.
3. Meanwhile, heat olive oil in a large skillet over medium-high heat. Add ground turkey to the skillet and brown well, crumbling as it cooks. Drain excess grease.
4. Add celery, onion, and garlic, and sauté for 3 minutes, just until celery begins to soften. Stir in tomato sauce, tomato paste, salt, and pepper, and bring to a simmer to finish meat sauce.
5. In a large mixing bowl, fold together all Cheese Filling ingredients, using only 1/2 of the mozzarella cheese.
6. Ladle 1/3 of the meat sauce over the bottom of the prepared baking dish, then top with a layer of 1/2 of the sliced eggplant. Top the eggplant with 1/2 of the Cheese Filling. Repeat with 1/3 of the meat sauce, then remaining eggplant, then remaining Cheese Filling. Finish with remaining meat sauce and top with remaining mozzarella cheese.
7. Bake 50 minutes, or until the top is golden brown. Let cool 10 minutes before slicing.

POULTRY

Calories: 265 • Fat: 14g • Protein: 23.5g • Total Carbs: 10g - Fiber: 4g = **Net Carbs: 6g**

PREP TIME: 25 MIN • COOK TIME: 20 MIN • SERVES: 4

CHICKEN MARSALA MEATBALLS

As a chef, I've been cooking Chicken Marsala for decades. It was THE banquet recipe when my restaurants would cater large events, but for that same reason, it can seem a little dated these days. In this recipe, I've taken those classic flavors and presented them in a fun and new way—as a meatball dish made with ground chicken breast in place of chicken breast fillets.

SHOPPING LIST

MEATBALLS

1 pound ground chicken (see tip)
1 large egg, beaten
1/4 cup grated Parmesan cheese
1 tablespoon chopped fresh parsley
3/4 teaspoon salt
1/2 teaspoon black pepper

MARSALA

1 tablespoon olive oil
1 tablespoon butter
1/4 cup diced red onion
8 ounces sliced baby bella mushrooms
3/4 cup beef stock or broth
1/4 cup Marsala wine
1/2 cup heavy cream
1 tablespoon chopped fresh parsley

1. In a large mixing bowl, use your hands to combine all Meatballs ingredients. Form into 16 equal-sized meatballs.
2. Heat olive oil and butter in a large skillet over medium-high heat.
3. Add meatballs to the skillet and cook until lightly browned on all sides, about 8 minutes.
4. Reduce heat to medium. Add the onion and mushrooms to the skillet and sauté for 5–7 minutes, until mushrooms begin to brown.
5. Deglaze the skillet with the beef stock and Marsala wine, scraping any browned bits from the bottom of the skillet. Bring the sauce to a simmer and cook until reduced by 2/3.
6. Stir the heavy cream into the skillet and bring back to a simmer before serving topped with chopped parsley.

HELPFUL TIPS

Any ground chicken can be used, though I prefer ground chicken breast for these, as it has the same taste and texture as fresh chicken breast. Use regular ground chicken for a softer texture.

Calories: 360 • Fat: 18g • Protein: 32g • Total Carbs: 4.5g - Fiber: 1g = Net Carbs: 3.5g

POULTRY

PREP TIME: 5 MIN • CHILL TIME: 4 HRS • COOK TIME: 1 HR • SERVES: 4–8

ROASTED CHICKEN ON A BUDGET

Chicken leg quarters may be the most tender and flavorful cut of chicken you can buy, and even better, they're often the cheapest! This is exactly how I prepare them when I don't want to spend an hour in the grocery store and another hour doing prep-work. It's as simple and inexpensive as it gets.

SHOPPING LIST

4–8 chicken leg quarters

Salt and pepper

Garlic powder

1 (9-ounce) bottle Italian salad dressing (see tip)

1/2 teaspoon dried rosemary, optional

HELPFUL TIPS

Be sure to look for salad dressing without any added sugar in the ingredients. We like to use Newman's Own brand of Olive Oil and Vinegar dressing, as we've found that particular brand to have the least ingredients (and easiest to recognize).

1 Place chicken in a large food storage container, and generously season with salt, pepper, and garlic powder.

2 Pour dressing over chicken, and toss to coat. For even more flavor, add the dried rosemary. Cover and refrigerate at least 4 hours.

3 Preheat oven to 350°F.

4 Remove chicken from marinade and transfer to a roasting pan, spreading them apart to not crowd the pan. Drizzle each with a tablespoon of the marinade, then discard remaining marinade.

5 Bake 30 minutes. Baste the chicken legs with the juices from the pan.

6 Raise heat to 400°F and continue baking an additional 30 minutes, or until a meat thermometer inserted into the thickest piece registers 170°F.

Calories: 525 • Fat: 42g • Protein: 31.5g • Total Carbs: 2g - Fiber: 0g = Net Carbs: 2g

CHICKEN WITH BASIL CREAM SAUCE

In this recipe, chicken breasts are breaded in Parmesan cheese that cooks up golden brown before being smothered in a quick and easy basil cream sauce. For even more color and flavor, I like to sprinkle diced roasted red peppers over the top just before serving.

SHOPPING LIST

2 large eggs

1/4 teaspoon salt

1/4 teaspoon garlic powder

1 cup grated Parmesan cheese

1 teaspoon dried basil

1/4 teaspoon black pepper

4 boneless, skinless chicken breasts (see tip)

2 tablespoons olive oil

BASIL CREAM SAUCE

3/4 cup heavy cream

3 tablespoons chopped fresh basil

1 teaspoon minced garlic

Salt and pepper

HELPFUL TIPS

Thinner chicken breasts (around 6–8 ounces) work best in this recipe, cooking all the way through without burning the Parmesan breading.

1 Preheat oven to 375°F.

2 In a shallow but wide bowl, whisk eggs with salt and garlic powder to create an egg wash.

3 In a separate bowl, combine Parmesan cheese with basil and black pepper to create a breading.

4 Dip chicken breasts in the egg wash, flipping to thoroughly coat. Transfer to the breading mixture, and press the chicken into the cheese to ensure the breading adheres.

5 Heat olive oil in a large skillet over medium-high heat.

6 Place the breaded chicken breasts in the skillet and cook for 4–5 minutes on each side, just until the breading is golden brown.

7 Transfer the browned chicken breasts to a sheet pan and transfer to the oven. Bake 10 minutes, just until the largest piece reveals no pink.

8 Meanwhile, prepare the Basil Cream Sauce by adding all ingredients to a small sauce pot over medium heat and bringing to a simmer. Let simmer 5 minutes, stirring constantly, until cream has slightly thickened. Season with salt and pepper to taste. Serve ladled over the cooked chicken.

Calories: 405 • Fat: 24g • Protein: 49.5g • Total Carbs: 2g - Fiber: 0g = Net Carbs: 2g

PREP TIME: 15 MIN • COOK TIME: 20 MIN • SERVES: 4

CHICKEN PARMESAN BURGERS

This is a new take on two classic cravings by smothering ground chicken burgers with tomato sauce and melted mozzarella cheese. There's even Parmesan and additional mozzarella cheese cooked right into the burger patties to keep the chicken moist and flavorful.

SHOPPING LIST

1 pound ground chicken

1 large egg, beaten

1/4 cup grated Parmesan cheese

1 cup shredded mozzarella cheese, divided

1 teaspoon minced garlic

3/4 teaspoon Italian seasoning

3/4 teaspoon salt

1/2 teaspoon black pepper

1 tablespoon olive oil

1/3 cup thick prepared pasta sauce

HELPFUL TIPS

These are great served over romaine lettuce with a slice of fresh tomato, or try them served over zucchini noodles or spaghetti squash.

1 In a large mixing bowl, use your hands to combine ground chicken, egg, Parmesan, 1/4 cup of the mozzarella cheese, minced garlic, Italian seasoning, salt, and pepper. Form into 4 thick burger patties.

2 Preheat broiler to high heat. Heat olive oil in a large skillet over medium-high heat.

3 Add burger patties to the skillet and cook until browned and cooked throughout, 4–5 minutes on each side.

4 Transfer cooked burgers to a sheet pan. Top each burger with an equal amount of the pasta sauce, then pile an equal amount of the remaining 3/4 cup of mozzarella cheese over that.

5 Broil just until cheese is bubbly hot and beginning to brown, about 4 minutes.

POULTRY

Calories: 275 • Fat: 17.5g • Protein: 28.5g • Total Carbs: 2g - Fiber: 0g = Net Carbs: 2g

PREP TIME: 20 MIN • COOK TIME: 20 MIN • MAKES: 9 • SERVES: 3

"FAST FOOD" CHICKEN STRIPS

You can make these chicken "fillet" strips any day of the week. . . even Sunday. With a breading that has a hint of sweetness and a savory tang (that secretly comes from a dash of pickle juice), these are sure to beat those fast food cravings.

SHOPPING LIST

3 boneless, skinless chicken breasts

2 large eggs

1 tablespoon mayonnaise

1 tablespoon dill pickle juice

1 1/2 teaspoons sugar substitute

1/4 teaspoon onion powder

1 cup almond flour

1/3 cup grated Parmesan cheese

1/2 teaspoon pepper

Vegetable oil, for frying

HELPFUL TIPS

Thinner chicken breasts work best in this recipe. I've noticed that boneless chicken breasts are now sometimes as large as 12 ounces each! What are they feeding those things? For a monster cut like that, you should lay plastic wrap over the breasts and pound with a mallet or rolling pin until 1-inch thick, then cut into 4 strips rather than 3.

1. Preheat oven to 375°F. Cut each chicken breast into 3 strips, lengthwise.
2. In a shallow but wide bowl, whisk eggs with mayonnaise, pickle juice, sugar substitute, and onion powder.
3. In a separate bowl, combine almond flour with Parmesan cheese and pepper to create a breading.
4. Dip chicken strips in the egg wash, flipping to thoroughly coat. Transfer to the breading mixture and press the chicken into the mixture to ensure the breading adheres.
5. Place a 1/8-inch layer of vegetable oil in a large skillet over medium-high heat.
6. Add the breaded chicken strips to the skillet and cook for 4–5 minutes on each side, just until the breading is golden brown. Transfer to a sheet pan.
7. Bake for 10 minutes, just until slicing into the thickest chicken strip reveals no pink.

Calories: 515 • Fat: 31g • Protein: 56.5g • Total Carbs: 9g - Fiber: 4g = Net Carbs: 5g

MEATS

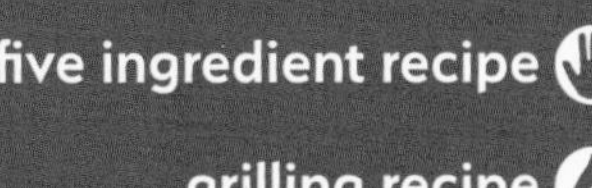

five ingredient recipe

grilling recipe

PREP TIME: 30 MIN • BAKE TIME: 50 MIN • SERVES: 8

SOUTHERN SHEPHERD'S PIE

While Americans have already Americanized this United Kingdom craving, I thought I'd take the dish down to the deep South. With smoky Gouda, yellow squash, green onions, and savory bacon, there's so much Southern flair that you'd never notice my sneaky substitution for mashed potatoes.

SHOPPING LIST

Nonstick cooking spray

1 tablespoon vegetable oil

1 1/2 pounds ground beef

3 stalks celery, chopped

2 cups chopped yellow squash

4 green onions, sliced

8 strips cooked bacon, chopped

Salt and pepper

8 ounces smoked Gouda cheese, shredded

MOCK MASH

24 ounces frozen cauliflower florets, thawed and drained

4 ounces cream cheese, softened

3 large eggs

1/4 teaspoon salt

1/4 teaspoon pepper

HELPFUL TIPS

For the best flavor, I like to mix a teaspoon of beef base (sold near the bouillon cubes) into the beef mixture before topping with the Mock Mash.

1. Preheat oven to 350°F. Spray a 13x9 or deep 4-quart casserole dish with nonstick cooking spray.
2. Heat vegetable oil in a large skillet over medium-high heat.
3. Add ground beef to the skillet and brown well, crumbling as it cooks. Drain excess grease.
4. Add celery, squash, 1/2 of the green onions, and 1/2 of the chopped bacon, and sauté for 2 minutes, just until squash begins to soften.
5. Remove from heat and generously season to taste with salt and pepper. Transfer ground beef mixture to the prepared casserole dish.
6. Meanwhile, prepare the Mock Mash by adding all ingredients to a blender or food processor, and processing until completely smooth.
7. Fold 1/2 of the Gouda cheese, the remaining green onions, and the remaining bacon into the Mock Mash.
8. Spread the Mock Mash evenly over the top of the ground beef mixture in the casserole dish. Top with the remaining Gouda cheese.
9. Bake 50 minutes, or until the Mock Mash begins to brown around the edges. Let cool 10 minutes before serving.

Calories: 430 • Fat: 31.5g • Protein: 30.5g • Total Carbs: 6g - Fiber: 3g = Net Carbs: 3g

 PREP TIME: 10 MIN • CHILL TIME: 1 HOUR • COOK TIME: 30 MIN • SERVES: 4

CILANTRO ORANGE PORK TENDERLOIN

This seared and then roasted pork tenderloin is rubbed with cilantro, onion, orange zest, and chili powder for both color and a tiny bit of heat. For a full meal, serve alongside my Sweet and Spicy Snap Peas, recipe page 148.

SHOPPING LIST

1 large pork tenderloin (about 1 1/4 pounds)

2 tablespoons olive oil, divided

1/4 cup cilantro, finely chopped

1 tablespoon minced red onion

2 teaspoons orange zest

1 teaspoon chili powder

1 teaspoon sugar substitute (see tip)

1/2 teaspoon salt

1/2 teaspoon pepper

HELPFUL TIPS

The small amount of sugar substitute in this recipe helps balance out the acid in the orange zest and heat in the chili powder, however, it can be omitted, if desired.

1. Rub pork tenderloin with 1 tablespoon of the olive oil and all of the other ingredients. Cover and refrigerate for 1 hour.
2. Preheat oven to 400°F. Heat the remaining tablespoon olive oil in a large skillet over high heat.
3. Place the seasoned tenderloin in the hot skillet and brown on all sides.
4. Transfer tenderloin to the oven and bake 20–25 minutes, or until a meat thermometer inserted into the thickest part registers 145°F
5. Cover and let pork rest for 10 minutes before slicing thin.

Calories: 270 • Fat: 12g • Protein: 37g • Total Carbs: 1g - Fiber: 0.5g = **Net Carbs: 0.5g**

PREP TIME: 10 MIN • COOK TIME: 15 MIN • SERVES: 5

SAUSAGE WITH SHAVED SPROUTS

Pre-shaved Brussels sprouts have been one of my favorite things to pop up in grocery stores in the last few years. They're not only convenient, they're absolutely delicious when sautéed in skillet meals like this one!

SHOPPING LIST

1 tablespoon olive oil

5 fresh (raw) links Italian sausage

1/4 cup water

1 (10-ounce) bag shaved Brussels sprouts

1 apple, cored and julienned

1 tablespoon balsamic vinegar

1 1/2 teaspoons sugar substitute

1/4 teaspoon crushed red pepper flakes

1/4 teaspoon onion powder

1/4 teaspoon salt

1/4 teaspoon pepper

HELPFUL TIPS

For a nice presentation, sausage can be removed from the pan and sliced after cooking.

1. Heat olive oil in a large skillet over medium-high heat.
2. Place Italian sausage in the hot skillet and brown on all sides.
3. Add water to the skillet, cover, and reduce heat to medium-low. Let simmer for 7 minutes, just until sausages are cooked throughout.
4. Add all remaining ingredients and stir fry for 3 minutes.
5. Cover and remove from heat, keeping covered for 3 minutes to steam, until sprouts and apple are crisp-tender.

Calories: 300 • Fat: 21g • Protein: 17g • Total Carbs: 10.5g - Fiber: 3g = **Net Carbs: 7.5g**

PREP TIME: 10 MIN • CHILL TIME: 4 HRS • COOK TIME: 1+ HR • SERVES: 4

CHINESE SPARERIBS

I crave the bright red spareribs you get from Chinese takeout restaurants, but sadly they are absolutely loaded with added sugar. My copycat recipe uses sugar substitute (of your choice) and only a few other ingredients to reinvent these ribs without those added carbs.

SHOPPING LIST

1 rack (about 3 pounds) St. Louis-style spareribs, cut into individual ribs

1/4 cup soy sauce

1/3 cup sugar substitute

2 tablespoons dry sherry wine

2 1/2 teaspoons five spice powder

1 teaspoon red food coloring, optional

HELPFUL TIPS

The red food coloring is entirely optional, but helps match the look of ribs that you'd get from a takeout restaurant.

1. Place ribs in a food storage container. Whisk together all other ingredients and pour over top, tossing ribs to coat. Cover and refrigerate at least 4 hours.
2. Preheat oven to 375°F.
3. Line a roasting pan with aluminum foil (for easy cleaning), then place a metal rack over top. Place marinated ribs on the rack and cover with aluminum foil.
4. Bake 1 hour.
5. Uncover and set broiler to high heat. Broil until ribs begin to brown, about 5 minutes.

Calories: 495 • Fat: 31.5g • Protein: 46g • Total Carbs: 3.5g - Fiber: 0g = Net Carbs: 3.5g

PREP TIME: 15 MIN • COOK TIME: 11 MIN • SERVES: 4

GRILLED CHEESESTEAK PACKETS

Rather than wrapping things in a starchy bread roll, this cheesesteak is packed into and cooked directly in aluminum foil packets. The high heat of a grill penetrates the foil to still get some color on the flank steak as it steams at the same time, keeping the meat moist.

SHOPPING LIST

1 pound flank steak, thinly sliced

1 bell pepper, thinly sliced

1/2 yellow onion, thinly sliced

1 tablespoon olive oil

1 tablespoon Montreal steak seasoning

4 slices provolone cheese

HELPFUL TIPS

Though there are a lot of different and more complex spices in Montreal steak seasoning, 3/4 teaspoon salt, 1/2 teaspoon pepper, and 1/4 teaspoon garlic powder can be used in its place.

1. Preheat an outdoor grill to medium-high, or an indoor grill to high.
2. In a mixing bowl, toss flank steak, bell pepper, onion, olive oil, and steak seasoning.
3. Lay out 4 squares of aluminum foil and top each with 1/4 the seasoned steak and vegetables.
4. Fold each piece of foil over and crimp the edges to make sealed packets.
5. Place packets on grill, cover, and let cook 10 minutes.
6. Open packets and top each with a slice of provolone cheese. Cover grill and cook 1 additional minute, just until cheese melts. Serve immediately.

Calories: 410 • Fat: 25.5g • Protein: 39g • Total Carbs: 3g - Fiber: 1g = Net Carbs: 2g

PREP TIME: 5 MIN • COOK TIME: 10 MIN • SERVES: 2

PARMESAN-CRUSTED SIRLOIN STEAKS

These steaks may seem elaborate, but there's no saying that cooking for a special occasion has to be an ordeal. Made with only a few pantry ingredients, the Parmesan topping on these tender sirloin filets is simple but certainly not forgettable.

SHOPPING LIST

1 tablespoon vegetable oil
2 top sirloin filets (6-8 ounces each)
Salt and pepper
1/4 cup grated Parmesan cheese
2 tablespoons mayonnaise
1 tablespoon butter, softened
1/2 teaspoon minced garlic
2 sprigs fresh thyme

HELPFUL TIPS

For more color, mix a tablespoon of chopped fresh parsley into the Parmesan Crust before broiling.

1. Place oven rack at the second-highest position, and set broiler to high.
2. Heat oil in a large skillet over medium-high heat, until nearly smoking hot.
3. Generously season sirloin filets with salt and pepper before adding to the hot skillet.
4. Brown steaks well, about 3 minutes on each side. For medium-rare, a meat thermometer stuck into the thickest steak should read about 125°F at this stage of cooking.
5. Meanwhile, in a small bowl, use a fork to whisk together Parmesan cheese, mayonnaise, butter, and garlic to create the Parmesan Crust.
6. Spread the Parmesan Crust evenly over the two steaks.
7. Broil steaks for 2–3 minutes, just until the Parmesan Crust is golden brown. Top each steak with a sprig of fresh thyme. Let rest 5 minutes before serving.

MEATS

Calories: 580 • Fat: 37.5g • Protein: 57.5g • Total Carbs: 0g - Fiber: 0g = Net Carbs: 0g

PREP TIME: 10 MIN • COOK TIME: 15 MIN • SERVES: 4

PORK CHOPS WITH APPLES AND SAGE

Everyone knows that apples and pork chops are the best of friends, and in moderation, apples can be low-carb friendly as well. This recipe uses only a single apple, sliced thin to spread all that friendship around!

SHOPPING LIST

1 tablespoon vegetable oil

4 (1-inch thick) boneless pork loin chops

Salt and pepper

Onion powder

1 apple, cored and thinly sliced

1/3 cup thinly sliced yellow onion

2 tablespoons chopped fresh sage

1 teaspoon cider vinegar

1/2 teaspoon sugar substitute

1/4 teaspoon salt

1/4 teaspoon pepper

2 tablespoons butter

HELPFUL TIPS

Be sure to slice into the thickest chop to check for doneness before serving. For particularly thick chops, transfer to a 350°F oven as you sauté the apples to ensure the pork cooks all the way through.

1. Heat oil in a large skillet over medium-high heat, until nearly smoking hot.
2. Generously season pork chops with salt, pepper, and onion powder. Add the seasoned pork chops to the hot skillet and brown well, about 4 minutes on each side. Remove from pan and let rest under aluminum foil.
3. Reduce heat to medium and add sliced apple, onion, sage, vinegar, sugar substitute, salt and pepper.
4. Sauté the apples and onions until apples are tender and onions begin to caramelize, about 5 minutes.
5. Remove from heat and return pork chops from the pan, tossing with the apples and onions before serving.

Calories: 360 • Fat: 15.5g • Protein: 45g • Total Carbs: 9g - Fiber: 2g = Net Carbs: 7g

PREP TIME: 10 MIN • COOK TIME: 8 MIN • SERVES: 4

GRILLED FLANK STEAK WITH ROMESCO SAUCE

Romesco is a thick sauce made from roasted red peppers and toasted almonds, ground together like a pesto. It goes perfectly over robust cuts of meat, like the simply grilled flank steak in this recipe.

SHOPPING LIST

ROMESCO SAUCE

1 (7.5-ounce) jar roasted red peppers, drained

1/4 cup toasted slivered almonds

1 tablespoon extra-virgin olive oil

1 tablespoon tomato paste

2 teaspoons red wine vinegar

1 teaspoon minced garlic

1 teaspoon smoked paprika

1/2 teaspoon salt

1/4 teaspoon pepper

FLANK STEAK

2 pounds flank steak

2 tablespoons olive oil

Salt and pepper

HELPFUL TIPS

You can also purchase pre-made Romesco sauce in jars in the Spanish food section of the grocery store, however, you should check for added sugars.

1. Prepare the Romesco Sauce by blending all ingredients in a food processor. Set aside until steak has been grilled.
2. Oil and preheat an outdoor grill, indoor grill, or grill pan to high heat.
3. Toss flank steak in olive oil and generously season with salt and pepper.
4. Grill for 4 minutes on each side for medium-rare. Flank steak gets tough if cooked to higher temperatures.
5. Let rest for 10 minutes before thinly slicing against the grain.
6. Serve the sliced steak smothered in the Romesco sauce.

Calories: 585 • Fat: 33g • Protein: 65g • Total Carbs: 4.5g - Fiber: 1g = **Net Carbs: 3.5g**

PREP TIME: 15 MIN • COOK TIME: 10 MIN • SERVES: 4

GROUND PORK STIR FRY

Using ground pork and fresh ginger in this simple stir fry makes it reminiscent of the filling of a Chinese dumpling (or potsticker as they are sometimes called). Broccoli florets, bell pepper, and red onion fill out the dish, making for a complete one-pan meal.

SHOPPING LIST

2 tablespoons vegetable oil
1 pound ground pork
Florets of 1 bunch broccoli
1 red bell pepper, sliced
1/3 cup diced red onion
3 tablespoons soy sauce
1 tablespoon grated fresh ginger
1 teaspoon minced garlic
2 teaspoons sesame oil

HELPFUL TIPS

1/2 teaspoon of ground ginger can be used in place of the fresh, but I'd highly recommend the fresh, as it has an entirely different flavor.

1. Heat oil in a large skillet or wok over high heat.
2. Add the ground pork and crumble it as it cooks, just until some pieces begin to brown, about 4 minutes.
3. Reduce heat to medium-high and add the broccoli, stir frying 2 minutes.
4. Add the bell pepper and red onion, and stir fry 2 minutes.
5. Add the soy sauce, ginger, and garlic, and stir fry a final 2 minutes, or until broccoli is crisp-tender.
6. Remove from heat and stir in sesame oil before serving.

Calories: 365 • Fat: 26g • Protein: 24g • Total Carbs: 9.5g - Fiber: 3g = Net Carbs: 6.5g

PREP TIME: 25 MIN • COOK TIME: 1+ HR • SERVES: 6

FAJITA MEATLOAF

With this recipe I've taken two of the foods that everyone craves and combined them into one low-carb crowd pleaser. There's just a tiny bit of heat from jalapeño and chili powder, but a whole lot of flavor.

SHOPPING LIST

Nonstick cooking spray

MEATLOAF

2 pounds ground beef (15–25% fat content)

1 cup shredded sharp Cheddar cheese

2 large eggs, beaten

1/4 cup minced red onion

1 jalapeño pepper, finely diced

2 teaspoons chili powder

1 teaspoon ground cumin

1 teaspoon salt

3/4 teaspoon pepper

TOPPING

1/2 green bell pepper, thinly sliced

1/2 red bell pepper, thinly sliced

Salt and pepper

1/2 cup shredded sharp Cheddar cheese

1. Preheat oven to 350°F. Spray a 9x5-inch loaf pan with nonstick cooking spray.
2. In a large mixing bowl, use your hands to combine all Meatloaf ingredients.
3. Transfer the meatloaf mixture to the prepared baking dish and use your hands to form an even top.
4. Bake 50 minutes.
5. Drain excess grease from loaf pan, then top meatloaf with the sliced peppers. Lightly season the peppers with salt and pepper before topping with Cheddar cheese.
6. Bake 20 additional minutes, or until a meat thermometer inserted into the loaf registers 155°F. Let rest at least 5 minutes before slicing.

HELPFUL TIPS

This is also quite good when made with shredded pepper-jack cheese in place of both measures of Cheddar.

Calories: 380 • Fat: 25g • Protein: 34g • Total Carbs: 3.5g - Fiber: 1g = Net Carbs: 2.5g

PREP TIME: 5 MIN • COOK TIME: 10 MIN • SERVES: 2

CRACKED PEPPER NEW YORK STRIPS

It's sort of a sin against the culinary gods to mess with a New York strip too much. You don't really want to cover up the flavor of the meat with a heavy sauce or too many spices. When it comes to great ingredients, the simplest preparations are usually the best. With only a cracked black pepper crust and a little melted butter over top, this skillet-seared New York strip is about as simple as you can get. . . And that's how it should be.

SHOPPING LIST

2 tablespoons whole black peppercorns

1 tablespoon vegetable oil

2 New York strip steaks (see tip)

Salt

2 tablespoons butter

HELPFUL TIPS

Look for New York strips that are 1 1/4 to 1 1/2 inches thick. For the best results, let them rest on the counter for 20 minutes before cooking.

1. Using a meat mallet or heavy rolling pin, crack the whole peppercorns into smaller pieces.
2. Turn on exhaust fan above your stove (the pepper will smoke). Heat oil in a heavy skillet over high heat, until nearly smoking hot.
3. Generously season steaks on both sides with salt, and then press into the cracked pepper.
4. Add the seasoned steaks to the hot skillet and let cook, undisturbed, for 3 minutes, until a crust has formed on the bottom. If the pan is creating a large amount of smoke at any time, remove from the heat for a few seconds to stabilize the temperature.
5. Flip the steaks and cook an additional 3 minutes to form a crust on the opposite side.
6. Flip the steak again and use an instant-read thermometer to check for doneness. Once it reaches 130°F, for medium-rare, immediately remove steaks from pan. For medium, let steaks continue cooking to 140°F.
7. Let steaks rest for 5 minutes before serving each topped with a tablespoon of butter.

Calories: 430 • Fat: 24.5g • Protein: 50g • Total Carbs: 3g - Fiber: 1g = **Net Carbs: 2g**

PREP TIME: 15 MIN • COOK TIME: 10 MIN • SERVES: 4

CHEESY HAM AND BROCCOLI SKILLET

Ham, broccoli, and cheese are a combination of ingredients that you can't help but crave! They also make for this quick all-in-one skillet meal that you can have on the table in under 30 minutes.

SHOPPING LIST

1 tablespoon butter
Florets of 1 bunch broccoli
1/3 cup diced yellow onion
1 teaspoon minced garlic
1/4 cup chicken stock
1/4 teaspoon onion powder
1/4 teaspoon salt
1/4 teaspoon pepper
16 ounces cubed ham (see tip)
1/2 cup heavy cream
2 ounces cream cheese
1 cup shredded sharp Cheddar cheese

HELPFUL TIPS

I like to buy actual ham steaks and cut them into cubes myself, as the pre-cubed ham sold in stores usually contains added sugar.

1. Heat butter in a large skillet over medium-high heat, until sizzling.
2. Add broccoli, yellow onion, and garlic to the hot skillet and sauté 2 minutes.
3. Add chicken stock, onion powder, salt, and pepper to the skillet and bring to a simmer. Cook, stirring occasionally, until liquid has nearly evaporated, about 3 minutes.
4. Add ham to the skillet and sauté 2 minutes, just until heated through. Broccoli should be crisp-tender; if not, continue cooking until it is.
5. Add heavy cream and, stirring constantly, bring to a simmer.
6. Remove from heat and slowly stir in cream cheese and Cheddar cheese, until entirely melted into the sauce. Return to the heat, stirring constantly, only for a few seconds, to ensure sauce is bubbly hot before serving.

Calories: 420 • Fat: 27.5g • Protein: 34g • Total Carbs: 9.5g - Fiber: 3g = Net Carbs: 6.5g

PREP TIME: 10 MIN • COOK TIME: 12 MIN • SERVES: 6

BRUSCHETTA LONDON BROIL

One of my favorite cuts of meat, London broil is grilled to perfection in this recipe, then topped with a homemade fresh tomato bruschetta (a lot like an Italian salsa) that is light enough to not overpower the natural flavor of the meat.

SHOPPING LIST

BRUSCHETTA

2 tomatoes, diced

8 leaves basil, thinly sliced

2 tablespoons extra-virgin olive oil

2 tablespoons minced red onion

1 1/2 teaspoons minced garlic

1/4 teaspoon salt

1/4 teaspoon pepper

LONDON BROIL

1 London broil (about 2 1/2 pounds)

2 tablespoons olive oil

2 teaspoons lemon juice

Salt and pepper

Garlic powder

Shaved Parmesan cheese, optional, to top

HELPFUL TIPS

Cooking London broil beyond medium is not recommended, as the meat will get tough.

1. Prepare the Bruschetta by placing all ingredients in a mixing bowl and tossing to mix. Cover and refrigerate as you prepare the steak.
2. Oil and preheat an outdoor grill, indoor grill, or grill pan to high heat.
3. Toss London broil in olive oil and lemon juice before generously seasoning both sides with salt, pepper, and garlic powder.
4. Place on grill, cover, and cook for 8–12 minutes, flipping 4 times to create crosshatched grill marks. A meat thermometer inserted into the steak should read 130° F for medium-rare, 145° F for medium.
5. Let rest for 10 minutes before thinly slicing against the grain.
6. Serve the sliced steak topped with the prepared Bruschetta and shaved Parmesan cheese, if desired.

Calories: 470 • Fat: 29g • Protein: 46g • Total Carbs: 3.5g - Fiber: 0.5g = Net Carbs: 3g

SEAFOOD

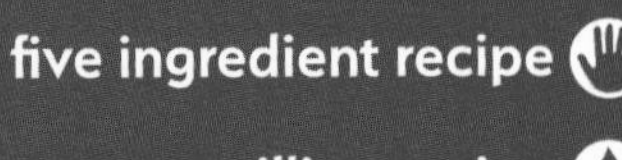
five ingredient recipe
grilling recipe

PREP TIME: 15 MIN • COOK TIME: 10 MIN • SERVES: 4

MOO SHU SHRIMP

When I crave Chinese takeout, I crave Moo Shu. With crunchy cabbage, earthy mushrooms, and scrambled egg, in a savory-sweet stir fry, this is the perfect combination of flavors and textures... Plus, it really lets the natural sweetness of the shrimp shine.

SHOPPING LIST

2 tablespoons vegetable oil

1 (16-ounce) bag shredded coleslaw mix

8 ounces sliced baby bella mushrooms

1 pound large shrimp, peeled and deveined

1 large egg, beaten

3 tablespoons soy sauce

1 1/2 tablespoons sugar substitute

2 teaspoons rice wine vinegar

2 teaspoons minced garlic

1/4 teaspoon white pepper

1/4 teaspoon five spice powder

1/4 cup sliced green onions

2 teaspoons sesame oil

HELPFUL TIPS

Moo Shu is traditionally served with thin flour tortilla-like "pancakes"—for a low-carb alternative, serve with lightly steamed cabbage leaves to use as soft wraps. If serving as wraps, be sure to remove the shrimp tails before cooking.

1. Heat oil in a large skillet or wok over high heat.
2. Add the coleslaw mix and mushrooms and stir fry for 5 minutes, or until cabbage and mushrooms begin to brown.
3. Reduce heat to medium-high and add the shrimp, stir frying for 2 minutes.
4. Move all ingredients to the edges of the skillet to make a well in the middle. Add the beaten egg and quickly scramble until set, then stir fry the scrambled egg into the cabbage and shrimp.
5. Add all remaining ingredients and stir fry an additional 2 minutes, just until shrimp are opaque throughout and cabbage is tender. Serve immediately.

SEAFOOD

Calories: 235 • Fat: 11.5g • Protein: 23.5g • Total Carbs: 11g - Fiber: 4g = Net Carbs: 7g

PREP TIME: 10 MIN • COOK TIME: 15 MIN • SERVES: 4

TILAPIA WITH TARRAGON CREAM SAUCE

Tarragon is an often underutilized herb that goes wonderfully with fish, especially when added to the white wine cream sauce in this recipe. I cook quartered artichoke hearts into the sauce for an even better presentation, with more texture and variety on the plate.

SHOPPING LIST

2 tablespoons olive oil

4 tilapia fillets

Salt and pepper

1/4 cup diced yellow onion

1/4 cup dry white wine

1 (14-ounce) can quartered artichoke hearts, drained

3/4 cup heavy cream

1 tablespoon chopped fresh tarragon

HELPFUL TIPS

The artichoke hearts in this recipe can be omitted if you'd prefer to make only the fish and the sauce, but they go very well with the tarragon and cream and make the dish feel more complete.

1. Heat olive oil in a large sauté pan over medium-high heat.
2. Lightly season the tilapia with salt and pepper. Place fillets into the hot pan and let sear for 3 minutes without moving the fish.
3. Flip tilapia and let cook 2 additional minutes, or until fish is flaky. Remove from pan and cover with aluminum foil.
4. Add onion to the skillet and sauté 2 minutes, just until translucent. Deglaze the pan by adding the white wine and bringing up to a rapid simmer.
5. Reduce heat to medium-low and add artichoke hearts, heavy cream, and tarragon to the skillet. Bring to a slow simmer, and cook, stirring constantly, for 5 minutes, until cream has slightly thickened.
6. Season sauce to taste with salt and pepper before serving over the cooked tilapia.

Calories: 320 • Fat: 17g • Protein: 33g • Total Carbs: 6.5g - Fiber: 2g = **Net Carbs: 4.5g**

PREP TIME: 15 MIN • COOK TIME: 10 MIN • SERVES: 4

GRILLED SHRIMP SCAMPI

Maybe the only thing that is harder to grill than shrimp is a buttery scampi sauce like the one in this recipe! I've made things simple by wrapping the whole dish in individual aluminum foil packets before grilling. You won't have to worry about shrimp falling through the grill grates, and you get to cook those shrimp directly in the sauce.

SHOPPING LIST

1 1/2 pounds large shrimp, peeled and deveined

5 tablespoons butter, melted

2 tablespoons white wine

Juice of 1/2 lemon

2 tablespoons minced red onion

1 tablespoon minced garlic

Dash Worcestershire sauce

1/2 teaspoon salt

1/4 teaspoon pepper

2 tablespoons chopped fresh parsley

1/2 teaspoon crushed red pepper flakes

1. Preheat an outdoor grill to medium-high, or an indoor grill to high.
2. Lay out 4 squares of aluminum foil and top each with 1/4 of the shrimp. Fold the edges of the foil up to create a bowl.
3. In a mixing bowl, whisk together all remaining ingredients, except parsley and pepper flakes.
4. Drizzle the scampi butter evenly over the shrimp in the foil bowls. Top with parsley and red pepper flakes.
5. Fold each piece of foil over and crimp the edges to make sealed packets.
6. Place packets on grill, cover, and let cook 10 minutes, just until shrimp are cooked through.

HELPFUL TIPS

This recipe can also be sautéed on the stove, all ingredients at once, for 5–7 minutes, just until shrimp are opaque throughout.

Calories: 260 • Fat: 16g • Protein: 27.5g • Total Carbs: 2g - Fiber: 0g = Net Carbs: 2g

PREP TIME: 10 MIN • COOK TIME: 15 MIN • SERVES: 4

"TOMATO PIE" FLOUNDER

Tomato Pie is a southern specialty with mayonnaise, cheese, and fresh sliced tomatoes. Here, I've taken all of those ingredients and used them to top flaky white fish fillets. Some tomato pie recipes use Cheddar cheese, while others use only Parmesan; I've stuck with the Parmesan in this, as it better complements the fish.

SHOPPING LIST

4 (6-ounce) flounder fillets
Salt and pepper
1/3 cup mayonnaise
1/3 cup grated Parmesan cheese
1 tablespoon butter, melted
1 teaspoon lemon juice
1/2 teaspoon dried thyme
1/4 teaspoon pepper
2 tomatoes, sliced
4 sprigs fresh thyme

HELPFUL TIPS

Any mild white fish, such as tilapia or cod, can be used in place of the flounder fillets.

1 Preheat oven to 425°F. Line a sheet pan with parchment paper.

2 Lightly season fish fillets with salt and pepper and place on the prepared sheet pan.

3 In a mixing bowl, whisk together mayonnaise, Parmesan, butter, lemon juice, thyme, and pepper.

4 Spread the mayonnaise mixture evenly over each fish fillet, then top with sliced tomatoes. Lightly sprinkle tomatoes with additional salt and pepper and top with a whole sprig of thyme.

5 Bake 15 minutes, or until topping begins to brown around the edges and fish easily flakes with a fork.

SEAFOOD

Calories: 320 • Fat: 22.5g • Protein: 26.5g • Total Carbs: 3g - Fiber: 1g = Net Carbs: 2g

  PREP TIME: 5 MIN • CHILL TIME: 15 MIN • COOK TIME: 8 MIN • SERVES: 4

CHILI-LIME GRILLED SALMON

If there's one thing we love more than grilling, it's salmon. It can really hold up to the bold flavors of chili and lime in this recipe's simple and quick marinade. Even when you include the time spent marinating, you can have this entrée on the table in only 30 minutes!

SHOPPING LIST

2 tablespoons olive oil

Juice of 1 large lime

2 teaspoons chili powder

1 teaspoon minced garlic

1/4 teaspoon salt

1/4 teaspoon pepper

2 pounds skinless salmon fillets

HELPFUL TIPS

I like to top this with a dollop of cilantro sour cream made by adding 2 tablespoons of finely chopped cilantro to 1/2 cup sour cream before seasoning to taste with salt and pepper.

1. In a food storage container, combine olive oil, lime juice, chili powder, garlic, salt, and pepper to create a quick marinade.
2. Toss salmon in the marinade, cover, and refrigerate 15 minutes.
3. Oil and preheat an outdoor grill, indoor grill, or grill pan over high heat.
4. Grill marinated salmon for 4 minutes on each side, or until it easily flakes with a fork. Serve immediately, alongside additional wedges of lime, if desired.

Calories: 420 • Fat: 23g • Protein: 52g • Total Carbs: 1g - Fiber: 0.5g = **Net Carbs: 0.5g**

PREP TIME: 15 MIN • COOK TIME: 10 MIN • SERVES: 4

JAMBALAYA SHRIMP AND SAUSAGE SAUTÉ

By omitting the rice, I've not only made this jambalaya-style dish low-carb, I've also made it super simple to prepare. You won't find traditional jambalaya cooked in only 10 minutes! For a complete meal, serve over cauliflower rice or zucchini noodles.

SHOPPING LIST

1 tablespoon vegetable oil

1 tablespoon butter

1/4 cup diced yellow onion

1/4 cup diced celery

1/4 cup diced green bell pepper

2 teaspoons minced garlic

8 ounces smoked sausage, sliced

1 pound large shrimp, peeled and deveined

Juice of 1/2 lemon

3/4 teaspoon paprika

1/2 teaspoon dried thyme

1/2 teaspoon dried oregano

1/4 teaspoon cayenne pepper

1/4 teaspoon salt

1/4 teaspoon black pepper

1/4 cup sliced green onions

1. Heat oil and butter in a large sauté pan over medium-high heat.
2. Add the onion, celery, bell pepper, and garlic and sauté 2-3 minutes, until vegetables begin to soften.
3. Add the remaining ingredients, except green onion, and toss to evenly coat shrimp and sausage with the spices.
4. Sauté for 5 minutes, just until shrimp are opaque and sausage is heated throughout.
5. Serve topped with the sliced green onion.

HELPFUL TIPS

For even more jambalaya flavor, add a fresh diced tomato when you add the shrimp and sausage.

Calories: 340 • Fat: 24.5g • Protein: 25.5g • Total Carbs: 5g - Fiber: 1g = Net Carbs: 4g

PREP TIME: 10 MIN • COOK TIME: 10 MIN • SERVES: 4

FORBIDDEN FRUIT SCALLOPS

While we all know that the apple is the "forbidden fruit," upon first discovery, grapefruits were dubbed that as well! I have no idea why, but I'm guessing it was because they were bitter? When cooking, you have to know how to work with that bitterness, and pairing them with naturally sweet scallops is exactly the ticket.

SHOPPING LIST

1 tablespoon vegetable oil

1 1/4 pounds sea scallops, patted dry

Salt and pepper

3 tablespoons butter

1/2 cup sectioned grapefruit

1/2 teaspoon grapefruit zest

1/2 teaspoon sugar substitute, optional

1/4 teaspoon salt

1/4 teaspoon pepper

2 green onions, sliced

HELPFUL TIPS

To almost entirely eliminate the carbs from this recipe, simply omit the sectioned grapefruit and increase the grapefruit zest to a full teaspoon for more grapefruit flavor.

1. Heat vegetable oil in a large skillet over medium-high heat, until nearly smoking hot.
2. Generously season scallops with salt and pepper and place in the hot skillet. Let scallops cook for 2 minutes on each side, moving them as little as possible. Remove from pan and cover.
3. Reduce heat to medium and add butter to the skillet. Cook, stirring occasionally, until butter begins to turn slightly darker in color.
4. Stir in seared scallops, grapefruit, zest, sugar substitute, salt, and pepper and let cook an additional 30 seconds, just until grapefruit is heated through.
5. Serve topped with sliced green onions.

Calories: 245 • Fat: 13g • Protein: 24g • Total Carbs: 7g - Fiber: 0.5g = Net Carbs: 6.5g

PREP TIME: 10 MIN • COOK TIME: 10 MIN • SERVES: 4

PROSCIUTTO-WRAPPED COD

This entrée is elegant, easy, and made with only a few fresh ingredients. By broiling, salty Italian prosciutto crisps right up around the tender and flaky cod, making for a marriage of flavors and textures that can't be beat.

SHOPPING LIST

4 skinless cod fillets
1 tablespoon olive oil
Juice of 1/2 lemon
Pepper
8 leaves fresh basil
8 slices prosciutto

HELPFUL TIPS

This is great when served topped with a dollop of an herbed cream cheese spread, especially Boursin brand.

1. Place oven rack 10 inches from broiler and preheat broiler to high heat.
2. Toss cod fillets in olive oil and lemon juice, then generously season with pepper.
3. Place 2 leaves of fresh basil over each cod fillet, then wrap in 2 overlapping slices of prosciutto, holding the basil in place. Place each wrapped fillet on a sheet pan seam-side down.
4. Broil 8–10 minutes, or until prosciutto is crispy and fish easily flakes with a fork.

Calories: 180 • Fat: 7.5g • Protein: 28g • Total Carbs: 0.5g - Fiber: 0g = **Net Carbs: 0.5g**

PREP TIME: 20 MIN • COOK TIME: 10 MIN • SERVES: 4

SHRIMP PRIMAVERA

Shrimp is sautéed with zucchini noodles, red onion, and cherry tomatoes in this fresh and colorful Italian entrée flavored with Basil, Parmesan cheese, and a hint of lemon zest.

SHOPPING LIST

1 tablespoon olive oil

1 tablespoon butter

1/4 cup diced red onion

1 1/2 teaspoons minced garlic

1 pound large shrimp, peeled and deveined

2 large zucchini, spiralized

1 teaspoon lemon zest

1/2 cup cherry tomatoes, halved

1/2 cup grated Parmesan cheese

3 tablespoons finely chopped basil

1/2 teaspoon pepper

1/4 teaspoon salt

HELPFUL TIPS

Florets of 1 bunch broccoli can be substituted in place of the spiralized zucchini noodles, although it is best to steam them until nearly tender before adding them to the skillet.

1. Heat oil and butter in a large sauté pan over medium-high heat.
2. Add the onion and garlic and sauté 2-3 minutes, until vegetables begin to soften.
3. Add the shrimp and sauté 2 minutes before adding the spiralized zucchini noodles and lemon zest.
4. Sauté for 4 additional minutes, just until shrimp are opaque and noodles are crisp-tender.
5. Remove from heat and stir in all remaining ingredients before serving.

Calories: 240 • Fat: 11.5g • Protein: 30g • Total Carbs: 8.5g - Fiber: 2.5g = **Net Carbs: 6g**

PREP TIME: 10 MIN • COOK TIME: 20 MIN • SERVES: 4

MAPLE BUTTER SALMON PACKETS

When cooking salmon wrapped in parchment, you're pretty much guaranteed to get perfect results every time. This simple preparation infuses the fish with sweet maple and a touch of nutmeg. While parchment paper makes for the best presentation, aluminum foil can also be used to make the packets.

SHOPPING LIST

4 (6-ounce) skinless salmon fillets

2 tablespoons butter, melted

1 tablespoon sugar substitute

1/2 teaspoon maple extract

1/4 teaspoon salt

Pinch nutmeg

HELPFUL TIPS

As nutmeg can be a strong flavor for some people, it can be omitted, if desired. I do recommend it though, as it is a complementary flavor to both the salmon and the maple.

1. Preheat oven to 350°F.
2. Lay out 4 squares of parchment paper and top each with a salmon fillet.
3. In a small mixing bowl, whisk together all remaining ingredients.
4. Drizzle the maple butter mixture evenly over each salmon fillet. Fold the parchment paper over and crimp the edges to create sealed packets. Transfer to a sheet pan.
5. Bake 20 minutes. Let rest 5 minutes inside the packets before serving.

Calories: 355 • Fat: 24g • Protein: 33g • Total Carbs: 0.5g - Fiber: 0g = Net Carbs: 0.5g

SLOW COOKER/ PRESSURE COOKER

five ingredient recipe ✋

PREP TIME: 20 MIN • COOK TIME: 8.5 HRS • SERVES: 6

BEEF BURGUNDY

I've written over a thousand recipes since my family began their low-carb journey, but I've somehow overlooked the quintessential French recipe—the recipe that made Julia Child famous—Beef Burgundy, or "Beef Bourguignon" as Child more appropriately called it. Simply beef stewed with mushrooms and pearl onions in red wine, this is as classic as it gets.

SHOPPING LIST

4 slices bacon, chopped

1 (3-pound) beef chuck roast, cut into 1-inch cubes

Salt and pepper

8 ounces button mushrooms, halved

2 teaspoons minced garlic

1 cup Burgundy wine

1 cup beef stock or broth

2 tablespoons tomato paste

2 sprigs fresh thyme

1 bay leaf

1 1/2 cups frozen pearl onions

3 tablespoons butter

PRESSURE COOK IT!

The first 3 steps can be done directly in a pressure cooker. Cook under HIGH pressure for 40 minutes before letting the pressure release naturally. Bring sauce to a simmer, add onions, and let sauce reduce by 1/2 before adding butter.

1. Heat bacon in a large skillet over medium-high heat, cooking until crisp. Transfer cooked bacon to a slow cooker, leaving the grease in the skillet.
2. Generously season cubed beef with salt and pepper and add to the hot bacon grease in the skillet. Brown well on all sides, raising the heat to high if necessary.
3. Add the mushrooms and garlic to the skillet and sauté alongside the beef for 2 minutes. Pour in red wine and scrape the bottom of the skillet to deglaze.
4. Transfer the contents of the skillet to a slow cooker and stir in all remaining ingredients, except onions and butter.
5. Cover and cook on LOW for 8 hours.
6. Stir in pearl onions, cover, and cook an additional 30 minutes, just until onions are heated through.
7. Turn off heat and stir in butter before seasoning the sauce with salt and pepper to taste. Serve immediately.

Calories: 600 • Fat: 30g • Protein: 65g • Total Carbs: 6g - Fiber: 1g = Net Carbs: 5g

PREP TIME: 10 MIN • COOK TIME: 10 HRS • SERVES: 6

HONEY MUSTARD CORNED BEEF

Few venture away from the pickling spice packet that comes with every cut of corned beef, but this recipe proves that there are delicious alternatives waiting to be discovered. I like to use whole grain mustard to crust the beef (the kind of mustard where you can see the individual seeds in the jar) as it isn't as spicy as Dijon or bold deli mustards.

SHOPPING LIST

1 flat-cut corned beef (about 3.5 pounds)

1 teaspoon pepper

1 tablespoon vegetable oil

1/3 cup whole grain mustard

3 tablespoons sugar substitute

PRESSURE COOK IT!

Add 1 cup of water or chicken stock to the cooker before placing the mustard-crusted corned beef over top. Cook under HIGH pressure for 80 minutes before letting the pressure release naturally.

1. Rinse corned beef well and pat dry with paper towels. Discard the spice packet that comes alongside it, instead seasoning the beef generously with the teaspoon of pepper.
2. Heat vegetable oil in a skillet over high heat. Add the seasoned corned beef and brown well on both sides. Transfer to a slow cooker.
3. Whisk together the mustard and sugar substitute before spreading over the corned beef in the slow cooker.
4. Cover and cook on LOW for 8–10 hours, or until meat is fork-tender. Remove from slow cooker and let rest 10 minutes before thinly slicing against the grain.

Calories: 480 • Fat: 35g • Protein: 35g • Total Carbs: 1g - Fiber: 0g = Net Carbs: 1g

PREP TIME: 30 MIN • COOK TIME: 8 HRS • SERVES: 6

GROUND CHICKEN CHILI

Even after slow cooking all day, this chili is lighter and somewhat fresher tasting than your typical chili made from ground beef. I like to serve it topped only with sour cream and fresh chopped cilantro. To brighten up the flavors, I squeeze a bit of lime over top of that.

SHOPPING LIST

1 tablespoon olive oil

2 pounds lean ground chicken

1 yellow onion, chopped

1 green bell pepper, chopped

2 tablespoons chili powder

1 tablespoon minced garlic

2 teaspoons ground cumin

1 teaspoon salt

1/2 teaspoon pepper

3/4 cup chicken stock or broth

1 (15-ounce) can black soy beans, drained

1 (14.5-ounce) can diced tomatoes, with liquid

1 (8-ounce) can tomato sauce

PRESSURE COOK IT!

The first 4 steps can be done directly in a pressure cooker. Cook under HIGH pressure for 20 minutes before letting the pressure release naturally.

1. Heat olive oil in a large pot over medium-high heat.
2. Add the ground chicken to the pot and crumble as it browns. Drain well.
3. Add the onion, bell pepper, chili powder, garlic, cumin, salt, and pepper to the pot, and stir to combine. Cook, stirring occasionally, for 5 minutes, just until onions sweat.
4. Pour the chicken stock into the pot and stir to catch any spices stuck to the pot. Transfer all to a slow cooker.
5. Stir all remaining ingredients into chicken and vegetables in the slow cooker.
6. Cover and cook on LOW for 8 hours, or HIGH for 4 hours.

Calories: 350 • Fat: 17g • Protein: 35.5g • Total Carbs: 13g - Fiber: 6g = **Net Carbs: 7g**

PREP TIME: 25 MIN • COOK TIME: 8 HRS • SERVES: 6

BRISKET WITH CARAMELIZED ONIONS

This simple preparation may seem too simple to be good, but the natural flavor of the caramelized onions that infuse into the meat during slow cooking truly don't need any extra help.

SHOPPING LIST

2 tablespoons butter

1 large yellow onion, thinly sliced

1 tablespoon vegetable oil

1 beef brisket (about 3.5 pounds)

Salt and pepper

2 cups beef stock or broth

1 tablespoon Worcestershire sauce

PRESSURE COOK IT!

Cook under HIGH pressure for 80 minutes before letting the pressure release naturally.

1. Heat butter and onions in a skillet over medium heat, sautéing until fully caramelized, about 15 minutes. Remove from skillet and set aside.
2. Add the vegetable oil to the skillet and raise heat to high.
3. Generously season brisket with salt and pepper and place in the skillet, browning well on both sides. Transfer to a slow cooker.
4. Add beef stock and Worcestershire sauce to the slow cooker. Liquid will not cover meat, but this is normal. Top the brisket with the caramelized onions.
5. Cover and cook on LOW for 8 hours, or until meat is fork-tender. Remove from slow cooker and let rest 10 minutes before thinly slicing against the grain.

Calories: 480 • Fat: 25.5g • Protein: 56g • Total Carbs: 3g - Fiber: 0.5g = **Net Carbs: 2.5g**

PREP TIME: 20 MIN • COOK TIME: 8 HRS • SERVES: 6

POT ROAST WITH SWEET POTATO GRAVY

The subtlety spiced and slightly sweet gravy in this pot roast is actually thickened with a whole sweet potato that has been cooked alongside the meat, then mashed. It's not only a "good carb" way to thicken a sauce (rather than using white flour or cornstarch) it's also more flavorful.

SHOPPING LIST

2 tablespoons olive oil

1 boneless beef chuck roast (about 3 pounds)

Salt and pepper

1 cup beef stock or broth

1 sweet potato, peeled and chopped

3 tablespoons minced red onion

2 teaspoons minced garlic

2 teaspoons Worcestershire sauce

1 bay leaf

1 teaspoon dried thyme

1/2 teaspoon allspice

2 tablespoons butter

1. Heat olive oil in a large skillet over medium-high heat, until nearly smoking hot.
2. Generously season chuck roast with salt and pepper and place in the skillet, browning well on both sides. Transfer to a slow cooker.
3. Add all remaining ingredients, except butter, and toss to coat meat in the spices before letting it rest atop the sweet potatoes.
4. Cover and cook on LOW for 8 hours, or until meat is fork-tender.
5. Transfer roast to a serving platter and discard bay leaf. Drain 2/3 the liquid in the cooker.
6. Using a potato masher, mash the sweet potato into the cooking liquid to create the gravy. Stir in butter before serving drizzled over the meat.

PRESSURE COOK IT!

The first 2 steps can be done directly in a pressure cooker. Cook under HIGH pressure for 80 minutes before letting the pressure release naturally.

Calories: 540 • Fat: 28g • Protein: 63g • Total Carbs: 5.5g - Fiber: 1g = Net Carbs: 4.5g

SIDE DISHES

five ingredient recipe ✋

PREP TIME: 20 MIN • MAKES: 12 • COOK TIME: 20 MIN • SERVES: 6

CLOUD BREAD

These fluffy bread rounds are like pure magic and make for great hamburger or sandwich buns. You can even spread dips on them like a pita bread, or use them as large chips when crispy and fresh out of the oven, as they do not soften until they cool.

SHOPPING LIST

Nonstick cooking spray

4 large eggs, whites and yolks separated

1/4 teaspoon cream of tartar

2 ounces cream cheese, softened

1 teaspoon sugar substitute

Pinch salt

HELPFUL TIPS

The texture on these is even better the next day, as they soften into true low-carb buns when stored in a covered container.

1. Place two oven racks in middle positions and preheat oven to 300°F. Spray two sheet pans with nonstick cooking spray.
2. In an electric mixer on high speed, beat the egg whites and cream of tarter at least 5 minutes, until stiff peaks form.
3. In a separate bowl, whisk together egg yolks, cream cheese, sugar substitute, and salt.
4. Gently fold the egg yolk mixture into the beaten egg whites, until all is incorporated into a batter.
5. Working quickly, use a large spoon to evenly drop 12 large rounds of the batter onto the prepared sheet pans. They should settle into a bun shape around 4-inches wide. The quicker you do this the better, as the batter will deflate over time.
6. Bake 20 minutes or until golden brown.
7. Remove from the pans and let cool completely before serving.

Calories: 80 • Fat: 6.5g • Protein: 5g • Total Carbs: 0.5g - Fiber: 0g = Net Carbs: 0.5g

PREP TIME: 5 MIN • COOK TIME: 5 MIN • SERVES: 4

SWEET AND SPICY SNAP PEAS

Snap peas are naturally sweet, but I add a little more sweetness and a lot of heat to make this delicious side dish. While I use soy sauce in place of salt, it is only to add more flavor, not to give these an Asian-flavor profile, so feel free to serve this alongside any meal of any cuisine.

SHOPPING LIST

1 cup water

1 pound sugar snap peas

2 tablespoons butter or margarine

1 tablespoon soy sauce

1 teaspoon minced garlic

2 teaspoons sugar substitute

1 1/2 teaspoons chili powder

1/4 teaspoon crushed red pepper flakes

HELPFUL TIPS

For even more flavor, I like to add in a tablespoon of minced red onion, but that's completely optional.

1. Bring water to a boil in a skillet over high heat.
2. Add snap peas to the boiling water, cover, and let cook 2 minutes. Drain well.
3. Add all remaining ingredients to the drained snap peas in the skillet and return to the heat.
4. Stir fry the snap peas for 2 minutes, or until crisp-tender. Serve immediately.

Calories: 105 • Fat: 6g • Protein: 3.5g • Total Carbs: 10g - Fiber: 3.5g = **Net Carbs: 6.5g**

PREP TIME: 10 MIN • COOK TIME: 7 MIN • SERVES: 4

BLACK AND BLUE ASPARAGUS

For a side dish that is full of flavor, asparagus is seasoned with a Cajun blackening spice and seared over high heat before being topped with cooling blue cheese crumbles.

SHOPPING LIST

1 pound asparagus, 2-inches trimmed from stalks

2 tablespoons vegetable oil, divided

1 teaspoon paprika

1/2 teaspoon salt

1/2 teaspoon pepper

1/4 teaspoon dried thyme

1/8 teaspoon cayenne pepper

1/8 teaspoon white pepper

2/3 cup crumbled blue cheese

HELPFUL TIPS

Be sure to turn the vent on over your stove before preparing these, as the spices cooking at high heat will create a lot of smoke... This is entirely normal.

1. In a large mixing bowl, toss asparagus with 1 tablespoon of the vegetable oil and all of the paprika, salt, pepper, thyme, cayenne, and white pepper, evenly coating the stalks with spices.
2. Place the remaining tablespoon of vegetable oil in a skillet over medium-high heat.
3. Add the seasoned asparagus to the skillet and cover. Let cook 5 minutes, only uncovering to occasionally stir.
4. Remove from heat and leave covered an additional 2 minutes, or until asparagus are crisp-tender.
5. Serve topped with the crumbled blue cheese.

SIDES

Calories: 165 • Fat: 13.5g • Protein: 7.5g • Total Carbs: 5g - Fiber: 2.5g = Net Carbs: 2.5g

PREP TIME: 10 MIN • COOK TIME: 5 MIN • SERVES: 4

SESAME PEANUT GREEN BEANS

These simple green beans are steamed and then stir-fried in the same skillet, leaving you with plenty of room on the stove to cook up an Asian entrée to accompany them. Nutty sesame oil perfectly complements roasted peanuts, both of which are added right at the end to keep their flavors rich and pronounced.

SHOPPING LIST

1 cup water

1 pound green beans, ends snapped

1 tablespoon vegetable oil

2 tablespoons diced red bell pepper

1 tablespoon soy sauce

2 teaspoons sesame oil

1/4 cup roasted peanuts

HELPFUL TIPS

These are also great with just a teaspoon of sugar substitute to add a little sweetness to offset the soy sauce.

1. Bring water to a boil in a skillet over high heat.
2. Add green beans to the boiling water, cover, and let cook 2 minutes. Drain well.
3. Add vegetable oil and red bell pepper to the skillet and return to the heat. Stir fry the green beans for 2 minutes, or until crisp-tender and beginning to brown.
4. Remove from heat and stir in soy sauce, sesame oil, and peanuts before serving.

Calories: 140 • Fat: 10g • Protein: 5g • Total Carbs: 9g - Fiber: 3.5g = Net Carbs: 5.5g

"GARLIC KNOT" EGGPLANT

This preparation of eggplant tastes just like the garlic knots you would get at a local pizzeria, only with way, way less carbs! Unlike those pizzeria balls of dough, this is a side dish you can actually feel good about eating on the side.

SHOPPING LIST

2 medium eggplants, cut into 1-inch cubes

3/4 teaspoon salt

3 tablespoons olive oil

1/4 cup grated Parmesan cheese

1 tablespoon minced garlic

1/4 teaspoon pepper

HELPFUL TIPS

The salting process in this recipe helps to make the eggplant less bitter, while also bringing out some of the moisture to make for better roasting.

1. In a colander, toss cubed eggplant with salt. Let rest 30 minutes, until eggplant begins to sweat.
2. Preheat oven to 425°F.
3. Rinse the salt off the eggplant and pat dry with paper towels.
4. Toss eggplant in olive oil and spread out on a sheet pan in a single layer.
5. Bake 20 minutes, flipping halfway through.
6. Top with Parmesan cheese, garlic, and pepper and toss to fully coat eggplant.
7. Bake an additional 5 minutes, just until eggplant has browned and garlic is beginning to caramelize.

Calories: 115 • Fat: 8.5g • Protein: 3g • Total Carbs: 9g - Fiber: 2.5g = **Net Carbs: 6.5g**

LO-CARB MEIN

With more bite than spaghetti squash, zucchini noodles make the perfect stand-in for high-carb pasta in this re-creation of take-out lo mein. It's high on flavor and low on carbs!

SHOPPING LIST

2 tablespoons vegetable oil

8 ounces sliced button mushrooms

1/4 cup thinly sliced yellow onion

2 large or 4 small zucchini, spiralized

2 1/2 tablespoons soy sauce

1/2 teaspoon sugar substitute

1/4 teaspoon ground five spice powder

2 teaspoons sesame oil

HELPFUL TIPS

Ground ginger can be used in place of the five spice powder, though the five spice is a more rich and complex flavor.

1. Heat vegetable oil in a large skillet or wok over medium-high heat.
2. Add mushrooms and yellow onion and sauté 5 minutes, or until onions begin to brown.
3. Add zucchini and sauté 2 minutes, constantly moving the noodles around in the pan.
4. Add the soy sauce, sugar substitute, and five spice powder and sauté an additional 2 minutes, just until noodles have reached your desired consistency.
5. Remove from heat and stir in sesame oil before serving.

Calories: 85 • Fat: 6g • Protein: 3g • Total Carbs: 6g - Fiber: 2.5g = Net Carbs: 3.5g

PREP TIME: 15 MIN • COOK TIME: 10 MIN • SERVES: 4

HASSELBACK ZUCCHINI

I must have made a million hasselback potatoes in my years working in restaurants. It's a very "old school" way to prepare a potato, where the potato almost unrolls like an accordion. Here, I've applied that same kitchen technique to low-carb zucchini, then stuffed Cheddar cheese and bacon between each knife cut to replicate the flavors of a loaded baked potato.

SHOPPING LIST

4 medium zucchini

2 tablespoons olive oil

Salt and pepper

Onion powder

3/4 cup shredded sharp Cheddar cheese

4 slices bacon, cooked and crumbled

1 tablespoon chopped chives

HELPFUL TIPS

The easiest way to cut these is to line a chopstick on either side of the whole zucchini before slicing. This way, as you slice, the chopsticks will stop your knife from cutting all the way through the zucchini.

1. Preheat oven to 425°F. Line a sheet pan with aluminum foil.
2. Slice ends from zucchini and discard. Carefully slice the zucchini only 3/4 of the way through, making slices every 1/4 inch. You should be able to fan the zucchini out when finished, with the bottom holding the whole zucchini together.
3. Roll the cut zucchini in olive oil to coat on all sides, then generously season with salt, pepper, and onion powder.
4. Fan each zucchini out and sprinkle Cheddar cheese and crumbled bacon between the individual slices.
5. Bake 10 minutes, just until zucchini is tender and cheese is bubbly hot. Serve sprinkled with chopped chives.

Calories: 240 • Fat: 20g • Protein: 10.5g • Total Carbs: 7g - Fiber: 2g = Net Carbs: 5g

PREP TIME: 15 MIN • COOK TIME: 30 MIN • SERVES: 6

WHITE CHEDDAR & BACON MOCK MAC & CHEESE

When it comes to cravings, macaroni and cheese has got to be at the top of the list! Sharp white cheddar and smoky bacon take my classic reinvention to another level—and green onions add just enough onion flavor to cut through the creamy sauce.

SHOPPING LIST

Nonstick cooking spray

1 large head cauliflower, chopped small

3/4 cup heavy cream

8 strips bacon, cooked and crumbled

3 green onions, sliced

2 cups shredded sharp white Cheddar cheese, divided

2 ounces cream cheese

1/2 teaspoon ground mustard

1/4 teaspoon salt

1/4 teaspoon pepper

HELPFUL TIPS

Okay to use 16 ounces of frozen cauliflower florets, thawed, in place of the fresh cauliflower, though it is recommended that you still chop the florets into smaller pieces.

1. Preheat oven to 375°F and spray an 8x8-inch baking dish with nonstick cooking spray.
2. Bring a large pot of water to a boil over high heat. Add the cauliflower and cook 5 minutes, just until crisp-tender. Drain well and pat cauliflower dry with paper towels.
3. Transfer cooked cauliflower to the prepared baking dish and top with bacon and onions.
4. Meanwhile, bring the heavy cream to a simmer in a saucepan over medium heat. Remove from heat and stir in 1 1/2 cups of the Cheddar cheese, all of the cream cheese, ground mustard, salt, and pepper. Stir until the cheese has fully melted into the sauce, returning to the heat only momentarily, if the cheese will not melt.
5. Pour the sauce over the ingredients in the baking dish and fold together to evenly coat the cauliflower. Top with the remaining 1/2 cup of shredded cheese.
6. Bake 20 minutes, just until sauce is bubbly hot and cheese is melted. Let cool 5 minutes before serving.

Calories: 360 • Fat: 29.5g • Protein: 17.5g • Total Carbs: 9g - Fiber: 4g = Net Carbs: 5g

PREP TIME: 15 MIN • COOK TIME: 25 MIN • SERVES: 6

BROCCOLI AU GRATIN

This broccoli casserole has a creamy Gruyere cheese sauce that reminds me of French cheese fondue (without the wine). It's then topped with a quick and easy low-carb breadcrumb topping for a bit more texture.

SHOPPING LIST

Nonstick cooking spray

Florets of 1 large bunch broccoli

1/2 cup heavy cream

1 1/2 cups shredded Gruyere cheese, divided

2 ounces cream cheese

1/8 teaspoon garlic powder

1/4 teaspoon salt

1/4 teaspoon pepper

Pinch nutmeg

TOPPING

3 tablespoons almond flour

2 tablespoons butter, melted

1 tablespoon grated Parmesan cheese

HELPFUL TIPS

This can also be made with a large (12–16 ounces) steam-in-bag of fresh broccoli florets, steamed in the microwave for 1 minute less than package directions.

1. Preheat oven to 375°F and spray an 8x8-inch baking dish with nonstick cooking spray.
2. Bring a large pot of water to a boil over high heat. Add the broccoli florets and cook 3 minutes, just until crisp-tender. Drain well and pat broccoli dry with paper towels. Transfer to the prepared baking dish.
3. Meanwhile, bring the heavy cream to a simmer in a saucepan over medium heat. Remove from heat and stir in 1 cup of the Gruyere cheese, all of the cream cheese, garlic powder, salt, pepper, and nutmeg. Stir until the cheese has fully melted into the sauce, returning to the heat only momentarily, if the cheese will not melt.
4. Pour the sauce over the broccoli in the baking dish and fold together to evenly coat florets. Top with the remaining 1/2 cup of shredded cheese.
5. Using a fork, whisk together all Topping ingredients until combined and crumbly. Sprinkle over top the cheese in the baking dish.
6. Bake 15 minutes, just until bubbly hot and topping is beginning to brown. Let cool 5 minutes before serving.

Calories: 265 • Fat: 22g • Protein: 12.5g • Total Carbs: 6.5g - Fiber: 2.5g = **Net Carbs: 4g**

PREP TIME: 10 MIN • COOK TIME: 10 MIN • SERVES: 6

HERB CREAMED SPINACH

Using herbed cheese spread not only makes this creamed spinach creamier, but allows you to pack it with more flavor using fewer ingredients. It makes the perfect side dish for heavily seasoned or spicy meats.

SHOPPING LIST

1 tablespoon butter

1/4 cup diced yellow onion

20 ounces frozen chopped spinach

1/2 cup (4 ounces) herbed cream cheese

1/2 cup heavy cream

1/4 teaspoon salt

1/4 teaspoon pepper

HELPFUL TIPS

Any flavor of cream cheese can be used, as long as you check the ingredients for added sugar. I like to use herbed cheese spreads like Alouette or Boursin brands, but Philadelphia brand makes a Garlic and Herb cream cheese as well.

1. Heat butter and onion in a large skillet over medium-high heat. Sauté 3 minutes, until onions are translucent.
2. Add the chopped spinach, cover, and let cook 5 minutes, stirring occasionally, until spinach has fully thawed.
3. Using a heavy spoon, press spinach and drain any excess liquid from the skillet.
4. Add cream cheese, heavy cream, salt, and pepper, and let cook, stirring constantly until the sauce is hot and bubbly. Serve immediately.

Calories: 135 • Fat: 12.5g • Protein: 3g • Total Carbs: 3g - Fiber: 1.5g = Net Carbs: 1.5g

PREP TIME: 20 MIN • COOK TIME: 5 MIN • SERVES: 6

FRIED OKRA

A Southern staple, Fried Okra is a side dish I've been meaning to reinvent for as long as I can remember. It was only after discovering just how versatile Parmesan cheese can be as a low-carb breading, that I was finally able to properly recreate these delicious and flavorful little bites.

SHOPPING LIST

2 large eggs
1 tablespoon water
3/4 cup grated Parmesan cheese
1/4 teaspoon onion powder
1/4 teaspoon pepper
2 cups frozen cut okra
Vegetable oil, for shallow frying

HELPFUL TIPS

Frozen whole okra can also be used for less pieces to have to bread before frying, though they will be less flavorful, with larger pieces of okra compared to the amount of breading around them.

1. In a shallow but wide bowl, whisk eggs with water to create an egg wash. In a separate bowl, combine Parmesan cheese, onion powder, and pepper to create a breading.
2. Dip each piece of frozen okra in the egg wash, flipping to thoroughly coat. Transfer to the breading mixture and press into the cheese to ensure the breading adheres to all sides.
3. For the best results, place the breaded okra in the freezer for 10 minutes before frying.
4. Fill a large skillet with about 3/4-inch of vegetable oil and place over medium-high heat. Let the oil heat up for about 2 minutes.
5. Place the breaded okra in the skillet and cook until golden brown, about 5 minutes, flipping halfway through. Do this in two batches if your skillet is too small. Drain on paper towels before serving.

Calories: 100 • Fat: 6g • Protein: 9g • Total Carbs: 3g - Fiber: 1g = Net Carbs: 2g

SNACKS

five ingredient recipe ✋

PREP TIME: 30 MIN • COOK TIME: 10 MIN • SERVES: 8

CRISPY ZUCCHINI PIZZA BITES

Crispy fried zucchini makes for the perfect crust in these party pizza bites that make for a great low-carb replacement for pizza bagels or rolls. That being said, this is like two recipes in one, as the fried zucchini is also great on its own, simply served with pizza sauce for dipping.

SHOPPING LIST

2 large eggs
1 tablespoon water
3/4 cup grated Parmesan cheese
1 teaspoon Italian seasoning
1/4 teaspoon pepper
2 zucchini, cut into 1/4-inch thick discs
Vegetable oil, for shallow frying
1/3 cup pizza sauce
2/3 cup shredded mozzarella cheese
1/4 cup mini or diced pepperoni

HELPFUL TIPS

Once the zucchini is fried, you'll want to quickly top them with the toppings to ensure that the breading doesn't sit too long, losing its crispness.

1. Preheat oven to 375°F. Line a sheet pan with parchment paper.
2. In a shallow but wide bowl, whisk eggs with water to create an egg wash. In a separate bowl, combine Parmesan cheese, Italian seasoning, and pepper to create a breading.
3. Dip each slice of zucchini in the egg wash, flipping to thoroughly coat. Transfer to the breading mixture and press into the cheese to ensure the breading adheres to both sides.
4. For the best results, place the breaded zucchini slices in the freezer for 10 minutes before frying.
5. Fill a large skillet with about 3/4-inch of vegetable oil and place over medium-high heat. Let the oil heat up for about 2 minutes.
6. Place the breaded zucchini in the skillet and cook until golden brown, about 5 minutes, flipping halfway through. Do this in two batches if your skillet is too small. Drain on paper towels and transfer to the parchment-paper-lined sheet pan.
7. Top each fried zucchini slice with a small dollop of pizza sauce, then a sprinkling a mozzarella cheese and a few pieces of pepperoni.
8. Bake 5 minutes, just until cheese has melted. Serve immediately.

Calories: 210 • Fat: 17.5g • Protein: 10g • Total Carbs: 4g - Fiber: 1g = Net Carbs: 3g

PREP TIME: 5 MIN • COOK TIME: 20 MIN • SERVES: 8

PUMPKIN PIE PUMPKIN SEEDS

Rachel and I always keep pepitas (shelled pumpkin seeds) in the house to top salads or green vegetables, but inevitably we end up snacking on them! With this recipe, we're encouraging snacking, by baking them with pumpkin pie spice, a hint of sweetness, and a hint of salt.

SHOPPING LIST

2 cups shelled raw pepitas (pumpkin seeds)

1 1/2 tablespoons butter, melted

1 tablespoon sugar substitute

1 1/2 teaspoons pumpkin pie spice

1/4 teaspoon vanilla extract

1/4 teaspoon salt

HELPFUL TIPS

Shelled pepitas can be bought in bulk at some grocery stores, but are often also available alongside dried fruits and nuts in the produce section. They may also be found in the Spanish foods aisle. If you can only find roasted pepitas, simply reduce the baking time to 5–7 minutes to cook the spices without burning the seeds.

1. Preheat oven to 300°F. Line a sheet pan with parchment paper.
2. In a mixing bowl, toss all ingredients until pepitas are evenly coated.
3. Arrange the coated pepitas in a single layer on the prepared sheet pan.
4. Bake for 20 minutes, stirring halfway through, until seeds begin to brown.

SNACKS

Calories: 175 • Fat: 15.5g • Protein: 7g • Total Carbs: 5.5g - Fiber: 1g = Net Carbs: 4.5g

PREP TIME: 10 MIN • COOK TIME: 6 HRS • SERVES: 16

BOILED PEANUTS BY THE BAY

Cooked up like a Maryland-style crab boil, these boiled peanuts are a crave-worthy snack that are worth the wait... The wait for them to finish boiling, that is! Plan on them taking all day to simmer to their savory and tender perfection and you won't be disappointed. There's really no way to overcook them and they only get better the longer you let them go.

SHOPPING LIST

24 ounces raw peanuts in shell

Water, to cover

1/4 cup minced yellow onion

2 tablespoons Old Bay seasoning

1 1/2 tablespoons minced garlic

1 tablespoon salt

2 teaspoons hot pepper sauce

1/2 teaspoon dried thyme

HELPFUL TIPS

This recipe calls for the type of raw peanuts that are sold dry and unrefrigerated, as they are more readily available. Refrigerated "green" raw peanuts can also be used by checking for doneness after only 2-3 hours of simmering.

1. Rinse the peanuts thoroughly before adding to a large stock pot.
2. Fill the pot with enough water to cover the peanuts by at least a few inches.
3. Stir in all remaining ingredients and bring to a rolling boil over high heat. Tightly cover and reduce heat to a simmer.
4. Let simmer 6 hours, or until peanuts are very tender. The liquid in the pot will likely evaporate as the peanuts simmer, so be sure to add additional water whenever necessary. Leftover boiled peanuts should be refrigerated.

Calories: 145 • Fat: 11g • Protein: 6g • Total Carbs: 5.5g - Fiber: 1.5g = **Net Carbs: 4g**

PREP TIME: 10 MIN • SERVES: 4

STROMBOLI ROLLUPS

Stromboli is a lot like a calzone stuffed with all different types of Italian meats. I've used those same meats here for these cold meat and cheese pinwheels that make a great snack or appetizer. For even more flavor, serve alongside pizza sauce for dipping, or drizzle with Italian submarine dressing.

SHOPPING LIST

4 slices deli ham (see tip)
4 slices provolone cheese
8 slices genoa salami
16 slices pepperoni
8 leaves fresh basil

HELPFUL TIPS

Rectangle or large oval cuts of deli ham work best to roll these up. We typically use rectangle cut "baked ham" sold in the packaged lunchmeat section.

1. Lay out the 4 slices of ham.
2. Top each slice of ham with a slice of provolone cheese, then 2 overlapping slices of salami, then 4 overlapping slices of pepperoni.
3. Top each stack with 2 leaves of fresh basil, then tightly roll each into a pinwheel.
4. Serve the rollups whole, or slice and serve as pinwheels.

Calories: 285 • Fat: 23g • Protein: 18g • Total Carbs: 1g - Fiber: 0g = Net Carbs: 1g

PREP TIME: 25 MIN • COOK TIME: 10 MIN • SERVES: 6

"MULTIGRAIN" TORTILLA CHIPS

Thanks to ground flaxseeds, these look (and taste) just like the fancy multigrain tortilla chips you'd see in stores, even though that is the only grain used to make them. The bulk of the chip is actually made up of almond flour in place of high-carb corn, but you'd honestly never guess it by the flavor and texture.

SHOPPING LIST

1 cup almond flour
1/3 cup flaxseed meal
1 large egg white, beaten
1 tablespoon water
1/4 teaspoon salt
Coarse salt, to top

HELPFUL TIPS

The thinner that you roll these out, the crispier these will be. I roll mine out until the dough is nearly transparent, however, thicker chips will still get crispy enough to dip, and that's all that really matters!

1 Preheat oven to 350°F.

2 Using your hands, kneed together all ingredients, until a dough has formed.

3 Split dough into two equal balls, then place each between two sheets of parchment paper. Use a rolling pin to roll each half of the dough out until it is very thin, about 1/8-inch thick.

4 Slice each sheet of dough into strips or triangles (strips are easier and taste just as good). Separate and transfer crackers to the prepared sheet pans.

5 Leaving the sliced chips on the bottom sheet of parchment paper, place on two sheet pans. Sprinkle chips with coarse salt, if desired.

6 Bake 8–10 minutes, until chips have crisped up and turn a very light brown. Let rest 10 minutes before serving.

Calories: 165 • Fat: 13.5g • Protein: 7.5g • Total Carbs: 7.5g - Fiber: 5.5g = Net Carbs: 2g

PREP TIME: 5 MIN • COOK TIME: 45 MIN • SERVES: 4

ROASTED ARTICHOKE HEARTS

By using frozen artichoke hearts, prep work for these tasty bites is a breeze. They actually roast up with a good crispness to them, making them sturdy enough to dip. See my Helpful Tips for a quick and easy Garlic Aioli dipping sauce.

SHOPPING LIST

2 (9-ounce) packages frozen artichoke hearts, thawed

2 tablespoons olive oil

1/4 teaspoon garlic powder

1/4 teaspoon salt

1/4 teaspoon pepper

HELPFUL TIPS

Make a quick Garlic Aioli dipping sauce for these by whisking together 1/4 cup mayonnaise, 1 teaspoon minced garlic, 1 teaspoon Dijon mustard, 1/4 teaspoon lemon juice, and salt and pepper to taste.

1. Preheat oven to 425°F. Line a sheet pan with parchment paper.
2. Pat thawed artichoke hearts dry with paper towels before tossing in olive oil, garlic powder, salt, and pepper.
3. Arrange the coated artichokes in a single layer on the prepared sheet pan.
4. Bake for 45 minutes, flipping every 15 minutes, until well browned. Let cool 10 minutes to further crisp up before serving.

Calories: 120 • Fat: 7.5g • Protein: 3g • Total Carbs: 10.5g - Fiber: 7.5g = Net Carbs: 3g

PREP TIME: 20 MIN • COOK TIME: 3 MIN • MAKES: 12 MIN • SERVES: 6

ROAST BEEF WRAPPED ASPARAGUS

Horseradish and green onion are made into a spicy cream cheese spread for these roast beef deli meat rollups. With a fresh and crisp asparagus spear poking out of each, these aren't just a quick and easy snack, they're also elegant enough to prepare for parties and entertaining.

SHOPPING LIST

12 large asparagus spears
6 ounces cream cheese, softened
2 tablespoons prepared horseradish
2 tablespoons minced green onion
Salt and pepper
12 slices deli roast beef

HELPFUL TIPS

Pencil-thin asparagus can also be used in this, though I would suggest preparing and using 2–3 stacked spears per rollup.

1. Boil or steam asparagus for 2–3 minutes, just until crisp-tender.
2. Transfer cooked asparagus to a bowl of ice water to stop the cooking process and cool them down. Drain and pat dry.
3. In a mixing bowl, whisk together cream cheese, horseradish, and green onion. Season to taste with salt and pepper.
4. Lay out the 12 slices of roast beef and spread a thin layer of the cream cheese mixture across the entire surface of each.
5. Place a cooked and cooled asparagus spear on one end of each piece of roast beef, then roll all the way up, using the cream cheese to hold the rollup together. Serve immediately or chilled.

Calories: 220 • Fat: 14g • Protein: 19.5g • Total Carbs: 4g - Fiber: 1.5g = **Net Carbs: 2.5g**

PREP TIME: 10 MIN • CHILL TIME: 12+ HRS • SERVES: 6

PICKLED GREEN BEANS

A real southern specialty, these pickled green beans make a great snack or chilled picnic side dish. Fresh dill and garlic add a ton of flavor to the brine, while crushed red pepper flakes add a bit of heat.

SHOPPING LIST

1 pound green beans, ends snapped

4 cloves garlic, halved

2 large sprigs fresh dill

1 teaspoon coriander seeds

1/2 teaspoon crushed red pepper flakes

1 1/4 cups water

2/3 cup white vinegar

1 tablespoon sugar substitute

2 teaspoons salt

1. Place green beans, garlic cloves, dill, coriander seeds, and crushed red pepper flakes in a food storage container or divide between two large jars.
2. Place water, vinegar, sugar substitute, and salt in a sauce pot over high heat and bring to a boil. Let boil 1 minute. Remove from heat and let cool 5 minutes.
3. Pour the vinegar mixture over the green beans and other ingredients.
4. Cover and refrigerate at least 12 hours before serving. Stores refrigerated for 1 full week.

HELPFUL TIPS

These are best around the second day of pickling in the fridge. Before that, they may be a bit crisp. After that, they may lose their bright green color, but will still taste delicious.

SNACKS

Calories: 30 • Fat: 0g • Protein: 1.5g • Total Carbs: 6g - Fiber: 2.5g = Net Carbs: 3.5g

PREP TIME: 5 MIN • COOK TIME: 15 MIN • SERVES: 8

SWEET BBQ PEANUTS

Most people don't realize how much sugar is in BBQ flavored potato chips and other snacks. Here I recreate that sweet and smoky flavor in a crispy coating around low-carb roasted peanuts.

SHOPPING LIST

1 large egg white

1 tablespoon butter, melted

2 cups shelled cocktail peanuts (roasted and salted)

1/4 cup sugar substitute

2 tablespoons smoked paprika

3/4 teaspoon onion powder

1/2 teaspoon liquid smoke

1/2 teaspoon pepper

1/4 teaspoon garlic powder

1. Preheat oven to 325°F. Line a sheet pan with parchment paper.
2. In a mixing bowl, whisk egg white and butter until frothy.
3. Add all remaining ingredients and toss until peanuts are evenly coated.
4. Arrange the coated peanuts in a single layer on the prepared sheet pan.
5. Bake for 15 minutes, stirring halfway through. Let cool 10 minutes before serving.

HELPFUL TIPS

If the roasted peanuts you use are only lightly salted, I would suggest adding 1/4 teaspoon more salt to season the egg white and cut through the other spices.

Calories: 195 • Fat: 16g • Protein: 8g • Total Carbs: 6.5g - Fiber: 3g = Net Carbs: 3.5g

PREP TIME: 25 MIN • COOK TIME: 12 MIN • SERVES: 8

NIPPY CHEESE CRACKERS

These Cheddar cheese crackers are sure to "nip" any salty-snack craving in the bud. While I've reinvented several types of crackers over the years, these are by far the closest to any store-bought cracker...in fact, they are nearly indistinguishable. I pull them out of the oven when golden brown, but the darker you bake them, the more they take on that browned cheese flavor that many people like in a cheese cracker, so try baking just a little bit longer, to see if you prefer them that way.

SHOPPING LIST

1 1/2 cups almond flour

4 ounces extra-sharp Cheddar cheese, grated

2 ounces cream cheese

1 large egg

1/2 teaspoon paprika

1/4 teaspoon garlic powder

1/4 teaspoon baking soda

1/4 teaspoon salt

Coarse salt, to top

HELPFUL TIPS

The cracker dough in this recipe is far easier to slice and separate into individual crackers when it is extremely cold. Simply place the rolled dough into the freezer for 5 minutes to chill before slicing. You can return the dough to the freezer if it gets too hard to work with.

1. Preheat oven to 400°F. Line two sheet pans with parchment paper.
2. Place all ingredients in a food processor and process until cheese has fully incorporated and a dough has formed.
3. Split dough into two equal balls, then place each between two sheets of parchment paper. Use a rolling pin to roll each half of the dough out until it is 1/4-inch thick.
4. Slice each sheet of dough into 1-inch by 1-inch-square crackers. Separate and transfer crackers to the prepared sheet pans.
5. Use a toothpick, or pointed-end of a chopstick, to poke a hole in the center of each cracker. Sprinkle crackers with coarse salt, if desired.
6. Bake 8–12 minutes, until the edges of the crackers are golden brown. Let rest 10 minutes before serving.

Calories: 210 • Fat: 18.5g • Protein: 9.5g • Total Carbs: 5g - Fiber: 2.5g = Net Carbs: 2.5g

SMOOTHIES & DRINKS

PREP TIME: 5 MIN • CHILL TIME: 1 HOUR • SERVES: 2

STRAWBERRY CEREAL MILK

Served ice cold, this milk tastes exactly like what is left at the end of a bowl of berry cereal. The secret is steeping freeze-dried strawberries and toasted almonds in the milk before serving. The almonds really give you the same nutty flavor of a toasted corn cereal.

SHOPPING LIST

1 3/4 cups unsweetened almond milk

1/4 cup half and half

1/2 cup freeze-dried strawberries

1/4 cup toasted almond slivers (see tip)

3 tablespoons sugar substitute, or to taste

HELPFUL TIPS

To toast almond slivers: Place in a heavy skillet over medium heat. Stir occasionally until golden brown and fragrant.

1. Add all ingredients to a blender in the order that they are listed, starting with the almond milk and topping off with the sugar substitute.
2. Pulse blender 3-4 times to break up ice before blending until mostly smooth.
3. Cover and refrigerate for at least 1 hour.
4. For a smooth texture it is highly recommended to run the milk through a fine mesh strainer or cheesecloth to remove all strawberry seeds and almond pieces.
5. Adjust sweetener to taste before serving.

DRINKS

Calories: 170 • Fat: 12g • Protein: 4.5g • Total Carbs: 13g - Fiber: 3.5g = Net Carbs: 9.5g

PREP TIME: 5 MIN • SERVES: 2

FROZEN STRAWBERRY COLADAS

Whether you prepare this frozen drink with or without alcohol, it makes for a refreshing getaway to enjoy on a hot day. Both coconut milk and extract pack a ton of tropical flavor, offset by sweet strawberries and a touch of lime for tartness.

SHOPPING LIST

1 1/4 cups unsweetened coconut milk

2 ounces white rum, optional

1 teaspoon lime juice

1/4 teaspoon coconut extract

3 tablespoons sugar substitute, or to taste

1 cup frozen strawberries

1/3 cup ice

HELPFUL TIPS

This can also be made as a virgin frozen "mocktail" by omitting the white rum.

1. For the smoothest consistency, add all ingredients to a blender in the order that they are listed, starting with the coconut milk and topping off with the ice.
2. Pulse blender 3-4 times to break up ice before blending until smooth.
3. Adjust sweetener to taste before serving.

Calories: 130 • Fat: 2.5g • Protein: 0g • Total Carbs: 10g - Fiber: 2g = **Net Carbs: 8g**

PREP TIME: 5 MIN • SERVES: 2

PEANUT BUTTER & JELLY SMOOTHIE

Frozen blackberries are the "jelly" in this protein-packed smoothie version of a childhood favorite flavor combination. Any mixture of frozen berries works well in this, though I find that blackberries taste the most like "peanut butter and jelly."

SHOPPING LIST

1 cup unsweetened almond milk

1/4 teaspoon vanilla extract

2 tablespoons sugar substitute, or to taste

2 tablespoons all-natural peanut butter

1 cup frozen blackberries

1/2 cup ice

1. For the smoothest consistency, add all ingredients to a blender in the order that they are listed, starting with the almond milk and topping off with the ice.
2. Pulse blender 3-4 times to break up ice before blending until smooth.
3. Adjust sweetener to taste before serving.

HELPFUL TIPS

For even more protein and a thicker texture, add 1/2 cup of silken tofu.

DRINKS

Calories: 155 • Fat: 9.5g • Protein: 5.5g • Total Carbs: 12.5g - Fiber: 5g = Net Carbs: 7.5g

PREP TIME: 5 MIN • SERVES: 2

GREEN GOODNESS SMOOTHIE

Fresh brewed green tea adds a unique flavor to this smoothie packed with honeydew melon, kiwi, and spinach. It's a gaggle of green ingredients that just so happen to be good for you to boot.

SHOPPING LIST

1/2 cup chopped honeydew melon

1 small kiwi, peeled

1 cup fresh spinach leaves

3/4 cup brewed green tea, chilled

2 tablespoons sugar substitute, or to taste

3/4 cup ice

HELPFUL TIPS

The green tea in this recipe is basically 1 mug of green tea, made from 1 tea bag. I like to let it steep for a full 5 minutes for more flavor. This is especially good when using a flavored green tea, such as peach flavor.

1. For the smoothest consistency, add all ingredients to a blender in the order that they are listed, starting with the melon and topping off with the ice.
2. Pulse blender 3-4 times to break up ice before blending until smooth.
3. Adjust sweetener to taste before serving.

DRINKS

Calories: 50 • Fat: 0g • Protein: 1g • Total Carbs: 11g - Fiber: 2g = Net Carbs: 9g

PREP TIME: 5 MIN • SERVES: 2

SPARKLING MELON ICE

Two types of melon are melded with watermelon-flavored seltzer water to make a refreshing and bubbly slush that is more of a dessert than a drink.

SHOPPING LIST

1 1/4 cups watermelon flavored seltzer water (see tip)

2 tablespoons sugar substitute, or to taste

1/2 cup chopped honeydew melon, frozen

1/2 cup chopped cantaloupe, frozen

3/4 cup ice

1. For the smoothest consistency, add all ingredients to a blender in the order that they are listed, starting with the seltzer water and topping off with the ice.
2. Pulse blender 3-4 times to break up ice before blending until smooth.
3. Adjust sweetener to taste before serving.

HELPFUL TIPS

Any flavor of unsweetened seltzer water will work well in this, but especially watermelon, if you can find it. Lemon is the second best choice.

Calories: 40 • Fat: 0g • Protein: 0.5g • Total Carbs: 8g - Fiber: 0.5g = **Net Carbs: 7.5g**

PREP TIME: 5 MIN • SERVES: 2

RASPBERRY CHEESECAKE SMOOTHIE

You could have a fruit smoothie, or you could have a fruit and CHEESECAKE smoothie like this one...I think we all know which one to choose! Without added sugars, you can feel good about drinking this dessert for breakfast, lunch, or even a snack.

SHOPPING LIST

1 1/4 cups unsweetened almond milk

1/2 teaspoon vanilla extract

1/4 teaspoon lemon juice

2 ounces cream cheese

3 tablespoons sugar substitute, or to taste

3/4 cup frozen raspberries

1/2 cup ice

HELPFUL TIPS

The lemon juice helps replicate the small amount of lemon added to a New York cheesecake, however, it can be omitted, if desired.

1. For the smoothest consistency, add all ingredients to a blender in the order that they are listed, starting with the almond milk and topping off with the ice.
2. Pulse blender 3-4 times to break up ice before blending until smooth.
3. Adjust sweetener to taste before serving.

Calories: 155 • Fat: 12g • Protein: 3g • Total Carbs: 10g - Fiber: 3.5g = Net Carbs: 6.5g

PREP TIME: 5 MIN • SERVES: 1

LOW-CARB BLOODY MARY

I've cut the carbs in this classic brunch cocktail in half by substituting vegetable stock for half of the tomato juice. I've also suggested V8 brand vegetable juice cocktail, rather than other tomato juices, as the mixture of vegetables has a few less natural carbs per serving than tomato juice alone.

SHOPPING LIST

Salt

3/4 cup ice

1/2 cup vegetable stock

1/2 cup V8 vegetable juice cocktail

1 1/2 ounces (1 jigger) vodka

1/2 teaspoon lemon juice

1/4 teaspoon Worcestershire sauce

Dash hot pepper sauce

Pinch pepper

1 stalk celery

Green olives

1. Salt the rim of a glass by moistening with water and then pressing into a plate of salt.
2. Shake together all remaining ingredients, except celery and olives.
3. Fill the prepared glass with fresh ice and strain the mixed cocktail over top.
4. Serve garnished with celery and green olives.

HELPFUL TIPS

For even more heat, add a bit of prepared horseradish to the cocktail before shaking.

DRINKS

Calories: 130 • Fat: 1g • Protein: 1g • Total Carbs: 7g - Fiber: 1g = **Net Carbs: 6g**

DESSERTS

LOW-CARB BROWNIES

Using creamy almond butter in these brownies helps to give you that chewy, fudgy texture you want in a great brownie, without using real sugar or milk chocolate. Using two types of unsweetened chocolate is a bit of work, but the results are more than worth the effort—these are real brownies, reinvented!

SHOPPING LIST

Nonstick cooking spray

1 ounce unsweetened baking chocolate

1/3 cup heavy cream

1/2 cup creamy almond butter

2 teaspoons vanilla extract

3 large eggs, beaten

2/3 cup almond flour

1 cup sugar substitute

1/4 cup unsweetened cocoa powder

1 teaspoon baking soda

1/4 cup butter

HELPFUL TIPS

Using baking soda in this recipe rather than baking powder helps neutralize the bitter aftertaste of unsweetened chocolate.

1. Preheat oven to 350°F. Spray an 8x8-inch baking dish with nonstick cooking spray.
2. Prepare a double boiler by filling a small pot with 2 inches of water and bringing to a simmer over medium-high heat. Place a stainless steel or tempered glass bowl over the pot.
3. Add the chocolate and heavy cream to the bowl of the double-boiler and mix with a silicone spatula, until combined. Remove from heat and stir in almond butter and vanilla extract.
4. Let the chocolate mixture cool 3 minutes before stirring in beaten eggs.
5. In a separate bowl, combine almond flour, sugar substitute, cocoa powder, and baking soda.
6. Fold the melted chocolate mixture into the dry ingredients before folding in melted butter to finish creating the batter. Evenly spread the batter into the prepared baking dish.
7. Bake 20 minutes, just until the center has set. Let cool at least 10 minutes before slicing into 12 rectangles to serve.

Calories: 160 • Fat: 14g • Protein: 4.5g • Total Carbs: 6.5g - Fiber: 2g = **Net Carbs: 4.5g**

PREP TIME: 10 MIN • BAKE TIME: 55 MIN • CHILL TIME: 4 HRS • SERVES: 12

COCONUT MACAROON PIE

This custard-based pie couldn't be any easier to prep—you simply throw all of the ingredients into a blender and blend, then pour it into a pie plate and you're ready to bake! It's almost magic and tastes like something you put far, far more effort into.

SHOPPING LIST

Nonstick cooking spray

1 1/2 cups unsweetened shredded coconut

1 1/2 cups heavy cream

2/3 cup sugar substitute

4 large eggs

2 large egg yolks

4 tablespoons butter, softened

2 tablespoons coconut flour (see tip)

2 teaspoons coconut extract

1 teaspoon vanilla extract

1 teaspoon baking powder

Pinch salt

1. Place oven rack in the center position and preheat to 350°F. Spray a 9-inch pie plate with nonstick cooking spray.
2. Add all remaining ingredients to a blender or food processor and blend until smooth and combined, but not entirely puréed.
3. Pour the batter into the prepared pie plate and bake 50–55 minutes, or until the center of the pie is browned and beginning to rise.
4. Cool on a wire rack for 1 hour. Cover and refrigerate for 3 additional hours before slicing to serve.

HELPFUL TIPS

The coconut flour helps set the final pie, however, this does work without adding it, the texture will just be a little more custard-like.

Calories: 175 • Fat: 15g • Protein: 4g • Total Carbs: 7g - Fiber: 2.5g = Net Carbs: 4.5g

PREP TIME: 35 MIN • COOK TIME: 18 MIN • MAKES: 10 • SERVES: 10

MATCHA TEA CUPCAKES

Japanese green tea powder, known as "matcha," is gaining in popularity as a unique ingredient for beautiful desserts. The powder is often sold near the boxed tea bags, but can sometimes be found in the ethnic foods aisle or even the baking aisle.

SHOPPING LIST

CUPCAKES

Nonstick cooking spray

4 large eggs

1/4 cup water

2 tablespoons butter, melted

1 1/2 teaspoons vanilla extract

2 cups almond flour

3/4 cup sugar substitute

1 1/2 tablespoons matcha tea powder

2 1/2 teaspoons baking powder

MATCHA FROSTING

8 ounces cream cheese, softened

1/4 cup butter, softened

3/4 cup sugar substitute

1 tablespoon matcha tea powder

1/2 teaspoon vanilla extract

HELPFUL TIPS

For an even more vibrant green color, add a few drops of green food coloring to the batter and frosting.

1. Place oven rack in the center position and preheat to 375°F. Line 10 cups of a muffin tin with paper liners and spray each liner with nonstick cooking spray.
2. In a mixing bowl, beat the eggs until frothy before whisking in water, butter, and vanilla extract.
3. In a separate bowl, mix the almond flour, sugar substitute, matcha powder, and baking powder.
4. Beat the wet ingredients into the dry ingredients, until all is combined.
5. Fill the prepared muffin cups with an equal amount of the finished batter, filling each about 2/3 of the way full.
6. Bake for 15–18 minutes, or until centers are firm and springy, and a toothpick inserted into a cupcake comes out mostly clean.
7. Meanwhile, prepare the frosting by adding all Matcha Frosting ingredients to an electric mixer and beating on high speed until light and fluffy.
8. Let cupcakes cool completely before frosting with the Matcha Frosting.

Calories: 320 • Fat: 28g • Protein: 11g • Total Carbs: 10g - Fiber: 4g = Net Carbs: 6g

PREP TIME: 20 MIN • CHILL TIME: 1 HOUR • MAKES: 16 • SERVES: 8

KEY LIME TRUFFLES

These truffles are like a key lime cheesecake, wrapped in rich dark chocolate ganache. To prevent melting, I serve them icy cold like a chocolate-covered ice cream bar.

SHOPPING LIST

FILLING

6 ounces cream cheese, softened

1/4 cup sugar substitute

1 1/2 tablespoons key lime juice

1/2 teaspoon vanilla extract

CHOCOLATE GANACHE

1 tablespoon butter

1/2 cup sugar substitute

2 teaspoons half and half

1 ounce unsweetened baking chocolate, chopped

1 teaspoon vanilla extract

HELPFUL TIPS

For even more zing, 1 teaspoon of key lime (or ordinary lime) zest can be added to the filling.

1. Line a small sheet pan or any freezer-safe dish with parchment paper.
2. In a mixing bowl, use a fork to whisk together all Filling ingredients. Form the mixture into 16 marble-sized balls. Place on the prepared sheet pan. Freeze for at least 30 minutes.
3. Prepare the Chocolate Ganache by filling a small pot with 2 inches of water and bringing to a simmer over medium-high heat.
4. Place a stainless steel or tempered glass bowl over the pot to create a double-boiler.
5. Add the butter, sugar substitute, and half and half to the bowl of the double-boiler and mix with a silicone spatula, until combined.
6. Add the chocolate and stir constantly, just until the chocolate has melted and all is combined. Remove from heat and stir in vanilla extract. Immediately prepare the truffles.
7. Using a fork, dip the frozen cream cheese balls, one at a time, into the warm ganache, spinning to coat. Work quickly before the chocolate cools. Place each coated truffle back onto the parchment-lined dish.
8. Freeze an additional 30 minutes, until the chocolate has hardened. Serve chilled or frozen, as these tend to melt quickly.

Calories: 120 • Fat: 11g • Protein: 2g • Total Carbs: 4g - Fiber: 0.5g = Net Carbs: 3.5g

PREP TIME: 30 MIN • COOK TIME: 10 MIN • CHILL TIME: 4 HRS • SERVES: 8

BUTTER PECAN SANDWICH COOKIES

Before I switched to a low-carb lifestyle, butter pecan ice cream was my absolute favorite flavor. Rather than do without, I've reinvented by making these chilled cookie sandwiches with that savory-sweet butter pecan flavor. I like to put them into the freezer for just a few minutes before serving to let them firm up into ice cream sandwiches!

SHOPPING LIST

2 ounces cream cheese, softened
2 tablespoons butter, softened
3/4 cup sugar substitute
1 large egg
3/4 teaspoon vanilla extract
1/2 teaspoon rum extract
1 cup almond flour
1/2 teaspoon baking soda
1/2 cup chopped pecans

FILLING

6 ounces cream cheese, softened
3 tablespoons butter, softened
1/2 cup sugar substitute
1/2 teaspoon rum extract

HELPFUL TIPS

While it is recommended to use unsalted butter in most baking recipes, using salted butter in this recipe works best for that true "butter pecan" flavor.

1. Preheat oven to 350°F. Line a sheet pan with parchment paper.
2. Place first measure of cream cheese, butter, sugar substitute, egg, vanilla extract, and rum extract into an electric mixer; beat on high, until fluffy.
3. Add the almond flour and baking soda to the mixer and beat until a thin dough has formed. Fold pecans into the dough.
4. Using a spoon or 1-ounce ice cream scoop, drop 16 evenly spaced dollops of the dough onto the prepared sheet pan, lightly pressing down to flatten into a cookie shape.
5. Bake 8–10 minutes, until cookies are set, but still springy in the center. Let cool at least 15 minutes.
6. Meanwhile, place all Filling ingredients into a clean electric mixer and beat on high, until well combined.
7. Spread a thick layer of the filling in between two baked and cooled cookies to make each cookie sandwich. Repeat with all remaining cookies.
8. Chill for at least 4 hours before serving cold.

Calories: 280 • Fat: 26g • Protein: 6g • Total Carbs: 5g - Fiber: 2g = Net Carbs: 3g

CARROT BAR CAKE

This double-decker cake is as delicious as it is impressive. As most of the flavor is in the spices, the actual grated carrot in this recipe can be entirely omitted to reduce the carbs without affecting much of the final flavor. For the best look, use natural almond flour (brown) with the hulls intact, rather than blanched (white) almond flour.

SHOPPING LIST

Nonstick cooking spray

CAKE

1 1/2 cups almond flour
1/2 cup chopped walnuts
2/3 cup sugar substitute
1 tablespoon pumpkin pie spice
1 1/2 teaspoons baking powder
1/8 teaspoon salt
4 large eggs
1/4 cup heavy cream
3 tablespoons water
1 teaspoon vanilla extract
1/2 cup grated carrots

CINNAMON CREAM CHEESE FROSTING

4 ounces cream cheese, softened
1/4 cup sugar substitute
2 tablespoons butter, softened
2 teaspoons heavy cream
1/2 teaspoon vanilla extract
1/4 teaspoon ground cinnamon

1. Preheat oven to 350°F. Spray an 8x8-inch baking dish with nonstick cooking spray. For the easiest release, then line the bottom of the dish with a square of parchment paper.
2. In a large mixing bowl, combine almond flour, walnuts, sugar substitute, pumpkin pie spice, baking powder, and salt.
3. In a separate bowl, whisk together the eggs, heavy cream, water, and vanilla extract.
4. Fold the wet ingredients into the dry ingredients until all is combined into a batter. Fold in grated carrots.
5. Spread the batter into the prepared baking dish. Bake for 40 minutes or until golden brown and a toothpick inserted into the center comes out mostly clean. Let cool completely.
6. Once the cake has cooled, prepare the Cinnamon Cream Cheese Frosting by beating all ingredients in an electric mixer on medium-high speed until smooth.
7. For a bar effect, cut the rounded edges from all four sides of the square cake (as in the picture).
8. Cut the cake in half to create two rectangles. Frost the top of one rectangle, then place the other rectangle over first for the second layer. Frost the top before slicing into 12 slices to serve.

Calories: 210 • Fat: 18g • Protein: 7g • Total Carbs: 7g - Fiber: 2g = Net Carbs: 5g

PREP TIME: 20 MIN • CHILL TIME: 30 MIN • MAKES: 12 • SERVES: 6

COCOA-NUT TRUFFLES

These Cocoa-Nut Truffles are made from unsweetened cocoa powder and chopped pecans, but also toasted coconut...which made me think; should I have named them Coconut Cocoa-Nut Truffles?

SHOPPING LIST

2/3 cup sugar substitute

1/3 cup unsweetened cocoa powder

2 tablespoons coconut flour

6 tablespoons butter, melted

2/3 cup unsweetened shredded coconut, toasted (see tip)

1/3 cup chopped pecans

HELPFUL TIPS

To quickly toast coconut, bake on a sheet pan at 325°F for 5 minutes, or just until golden brown.

1. Line a small sheet pan or any freezer-safe dish with parchment paper.
2. In a mixing bowl, use a fork to whisk together sugar substitute, cocoa powder, and coconut flour.
3. Whisk the butter into the dry ingredients until fully combined.
4. Fold the toasted coconut and chopped pecans into the chocolate mixture.
5. Using 1-ounce scoop or tablespoon, drop 12 rounded tablespoons of the batter onto the prepared sheet pan.
6. Place in freezer for 30 minutes before serving chilled or transferring to the refrigerator to serve later.

Calories: 270 • Fat: 26g • Protein: 3g • Total Carbs: 10g - Fiber: 5g = Net Carbs: 5g

PREP TIME: 15 MIN • COOK TIME: 50 MIN • SERVES: 6

PISTACHIO PUDDING CUPS

It's amazing just how much real pistachio flavor bakes into these creamy pudding cups. It tastes exactly like store-bought instant pistachio pudding mix, but without all of those fillers and processed ingredients!

SHOPPING LIST

Nonstick cooking spray

1/3 cup chopped pistachios

1 1/4 cups half and half

4 ounces cream cheese, softened

1 large egg

2 large egg yolks

1/2 cup sugar substitute

1/2 teaspoon almond extract

1/2 teaspoon vanilla extract

HELPFUL TIPS

To truly look like pistachio pudding, we highly recommend adding 6–8 drops of green food coloring to the pudding before baking.

1. Add 1 inch of water to a shallow roasting pan to make a water bath. Place on the center oven rack before preheating oven to 350°F.
2. Spray 6 small custard cups (ramekins) with nonstick cooking spray. Fill each with an equal amount of the chopped pistachios.
3. Place all remaining ingredients in an electric mixer and beat until fully combined.
4. Pour equal amounts of the mixture into the 6 prepared custard cups.
5. Place the filled custard cups directly into the preheated water bath. Bake for 45–50 minutes, or until set around the edges, but jiggly in the center.
6. Let cool on counter for 1 hour. Cover and refrigerate for an additional 3 hours before serving in the custard cups.

Calories: 190 • Fat: 16g • Protein: 5.5g • Total Carbs: 6g - Fiber: 0g = **Net Carbs: 6g**

PREP TIME: 15 MIN • SERVES: 2

CAPPUCCINO FREEZER-BAG ICE CREAM

What's not to love about homemade ice cream in only 8 minutes without the need for any ice cream maker? Instead, you make this ice cream by shaking the ingredients in a food storage bag, placed inside another food storage bag filled with ice and salt. It's a bit of a workout, but well worth the effort. We like to add chopped pecans to the coffee-flavored ice cream for a bit of texture, but this is entirely optional.

SHOPPING LIST

Quart-size and gallon-size freezer bags

1/3 cup Kosher salt

4 cups ice

2/3 cup heavy cream

2 tablespoons sugar substitute

1 teaspoon coffee extract

1/4 teaspoon vanilla extract

1/3 cup chopped pecans, optional

HELPFUL TIPS

This same method can be used to prepare vanilla ice cream by simply omitting the coffee extract and increasing the vanilla to 1 teaspoon.

1. Place salt and ice in a 1-gallon food storage bag.
2. In a mixing bowl, whisk together heavy cream, sugar substitute, coffee extract, and vanilla extract to create the ice cream base. Stir in chopped pecans.
3. Pour the ice cream base into a 1-quart-size food storage bag and seal the zipper.
4. Place the filled quart-sized bag into the ice in the gallon-sized bag and then seal the gallon bag.
5. Fold the tops of both bags over in your hand to reinforce the sealed zippers and shake the bags. Continue shaking the bags until ice cream is firm, about 8 minutes.
6. Use a paper towel to wipe any salt from the inner bag before opening the seal to serve. For firmer ice cream, place in freezer for 30 minutes before serving.

Calories: 290 • Fat: 29.5g • Protein: 3g • Total Carbs: 5.5g - Fiber: 2g = Net Carbs: 3.5g

PREP TIME: 15 MIN • COOK TIME: 12 MIN • MAKES: 16 • SERVES: 8

VANILLA MINT COOKIES

These cookies are a great after-dinner treat (especially around the holidays) with a flavor that reminds me of Andes Mints, even without any added chocolate! We like to add chopped pecans to them for more texture, but that is entirely optional.

SHOPPING LIST

1 cup sugar substitute

2 ounces cream cheese, softened

2 tablespoons unsalted butter, softened

1 teaspoon peppermint extract

1/2 teaspoon vanilla extract

10 drops green food coloring (see tip)

3 large egg whites

1 cup almond flour

1/2 teaspoon baking soda

Pinch salt

1/4 cup chopped pecans, optional

HELPFUL TIPS

The green food coloring in this recipe is entirely for looks and can be omitted. However, it does help to warn people that the cookies are mint flavored.

1. Preheat oven to 350°F. Line a sheet pan with parchment paper.
2. Add the sugar substitute, cream cheese, butter, peppermint extract, vanilla extract, and food coloring to an electric mixer set to low. Mix until blended. Raise the speed to high and continue mixing until creamy.
3. Turn the mixer back down to low and slowly add the egg whites.
4. Gradually add the almond flour, baking soda, and salt, and mix until just combined. Be careful not to overmix. Fold in chopped pecans.
5. Using a 1-ounce ice cream scoop or tablespoon, drop 16 rounded tablespoons of the cookie dough onto the prepared sheet pan. Tap sheet pan on counter to flatten out cookies.
6. Bake for 10–12 minutes, until edges of cookies are lightly browned. Let cool 5 minutes before serving.

Calories: 180 • Fat: 15g • Protein: 5g • Total Carbs: 7g - Fiber: 2g = **Net Carbs: 5g**

PREP TIME: 15 MIN • CHILL TIME: 4 HRS • SERVES: 16

DOUBLE PEANUT BUTTER FUDGE

While peanut butter fudge may seem like a no-brainer when it comes to low-carb desserts, it was actually much more difficult for me to reinvent than you'd think! With regular fudge, the sugar helps bind everything together, something that sugar substitutes are not very good at replicating. I found that the trick was adding powdered peanut butter (which is mostly peanut protein) on top of the regular peanut butter. The extra peanut protein, as well as added butter, really firms this fudge up when chilled.

SHOPPING LIST

Nonstick cooking spray

1 cup sugar substitute

1/2 cup (1 stick) butter, melted

1/2 cup powdered peanut butter (see tip)

1 (16-ounce) jar all-natural peanut butter

1/2 teaspoon vanilla extract

HELPFUL TIPS

Many brands of powdered peanut butter include a small amount of added sugar to offset the natural sugar that is lost when separating the protein into a powder. Thankfully, there are a few brands without any added sugar. I order a brand called "PB Naked" online.

1. Line the bottom of an 8-inch square baking dish or 9-inch loaf pan with parchment paper and spray with nonstick cooking spray.
2. In a large mixing bowl, whisk sugar substitute into the melted butter until fully dissolved.
3. Add the powdered peanut butter and whisk until smooth.
4. Add the regular peanut butter and vanilla extract and fold all ingredients together.
5. Spread the fudge mixture into the prepared baking dish, cover, and refrigerate for at least 4 hours.
6. Slice into 16 squares and serve very cold. If the fudge begins to melt, simply place in the freezer for a few minutes to cool down.

Calories: 255 • Fat: 20g • Protein: 8.5g • Total Carbs: 8g - Fiber: 2.5g = Net Carbs: 5.5g

PREP TIME: 20 MIN • BAKE TIME: 1 HR • CHILL TIME: 5+ HRS • SERVES: 12

STRAWBERRIES N' CREAM CHEESECAKE

Rachel and I have developed a lot of cheesecakes over the years, but this is an entirely new recipe for a 9-inch cake with thinner, longer slices and a strawberry flavor that tastes just like a strawberry milkshake! The cake is more dense and creamy (think Cheesecake Factory) thanks to using sour cream and fewer eggs than our traditional, fluffy ricotta cheesecakes.

SHOPPING LIST

Nonstick cooking spray

2 pounds (4 bricks) cream cheese, softened

1 1/2 cups sugar substitute

1/2 cup sour cream, room temperature

2 tablespoons strawberry extract

1 tablespoon vanilla extract

12 drops red food coloring, optional

3 large eggs, room temperature

1 large egg yolk, room temperature

HELPFUL TIPS

Strawberry extract can be found near the vanilla extract in many stores. We've found it at Super Wal-Mart.

1. Place oven rack in the center position and preheat to 325°F. Spray a 9-inch springform pan with nonstick cooking spray, then wrap the bottom of the outside of the pan with aluminum foil to prevent leaking.
2. Make a water bath by pouring 1 inch of hot water into a shallow roasting pan. Place the water bath onto the center oven rack to preheat.
3. Place the cream cheese and sugar substitute in an electric mixer and mix on medium speed, until creamy and combined.
4. Add the sour cream, strawberry extract, vanilla extract, and red food coloring, and continue beating, just until combined.
5. Add the eggs to the mixer one at a time, continuing to beat just until all is blended and smooth.
6. Pour the filling into the prepared springform pan. Place pan in the preheated water bath and bake for 1 hour, just until edges are pulling away from the sides of the pan and raising up, but center is still jiggly.
7. Turn oven off, open oven door 6 inches, and let cheesecake cool as the oven cools for 30 minutes.
8. Remove from water bath and cool completely on a wire rack before refrigerating at least 4 hours, until fully set. Slice into 12 slices to serve.

Calories: 330 • Fat: 30g • Protein: 8g • Total Carbs: 5g - Fiber: 0g = **Net Carbs: 5g**

Recipe Index

BREAKFAST

LUNCH

STARTERS

five ingredient recipe · grilling recipe

POULTRY

MEATS

SEAFOOD

Recipe Index

SLOW / PRESSURE COOKER

SIDE DISHES

SNACKS

five ingredient recipe (hand icon) grilling recipe (flame icon)

SMOOTHIES & DRINKS

DESSERTS

ALL GRILLING

ABOUT THE AUTHOR

George Stella has been a professional chef for over 30 years. He has appeared on numerous television and news shows, including two seasons of his own show, *Low Carb and Lovin' It*, on the Food Network. Most recently he appeared on *The Dr. Oz Show* for a profile on the comfort foods the Stella family reinvented using unique and low-carb alternatives to white flour and sugar.

Connecticut born, George has spent more than half of his life in Florida, where he lives today, with his wife Rachel. This is his ninth cookbook.

To keep up to date on George, please visit:
www.StellaStyle.com

ABOUT THE BOOK

The food photographs and design of this book were done by **Christian and Elise Stella**, George's son and daughter-in-law. They have worked previously on the design and photography of more than two dozen cookbooks for various authors. Christian is also a *New York Times* bestselling author for *Great Food Fast*, which he co-authored alongside Bob Warden.

All food in the photographs was purchased at an ordinary grocery store or grown in Rachel's garden. Dishes were prepared to the recipe's directions. No artificial food styling techniques were used to "enhance" the food's appearance.